CW00350876

Pattern Generation for Computational Art

Stefan Hollos and J. Richard Hollos

Pattern Generation for Computational Art
by Stefan Hollos and J. Richard Hollos
Paper ISBN 978-1-887187-18-3
Ebook ISBN 978-1-887187-19-0

Copyright ©2013 by Exstrom Laboratories LLC

All rights reserved. No part of this document may be reproduced or transmitted in any form or by any means, electronic or mechanical, including photocopying, recording, or by any information storage and retrieval system, without permission in writing from the publisher.

Abrazol Publishing

an imprint of Exstrom Laboratories LLC
662 Nelson Park Drive, Longmont, CO 80503-7674 U.S.A.

About the Cover

All patterns on the cover were created with the software accompanying this book. Cover design made with the help of Inkscape.

Contents

PREFACE

Creating beautiful images with math and computer programs has fascinated us since the early days of the fractal craze in the 1980's. The challenge of writing programs that implement mathematical algorithms, and then being rewarded with beautiful images is addictive. This also gives us the feeling of catching a glimpse of the platonic world of mathematics. Some people see elves and kaleidoscopic images when taking DMT (Dimethyltryptamine). Here you can create kaleidoscopic images using only a computer, and there are no elves to get in the way.

All the software used in the creation of the images in this book are free for readers to use and generate their own SVG images. It can be downloaded from the book's website at:
http://www.abrazol.com/books/patterngen/
The software consists of small programs written in the C programming language that can be run on all major operating systems. Inside the book are 327 images serving as inspiration for the kinds of images you can create. There are an infinite variety of images you can generate using the software that comes with this book, providing a computational image generation lab.

The origin of this book goes back to around 1990 when Stefan wrote up some notes on L-systems. He recently rediscovered the notes among his papers and we decided to combine them with some recent work that we have been doing in automaton theory and the combinatorics of words. What is really new in this book, in terms of computational art, is the use of Christoffel words and automatic sequences for binary string production, as well as the use of finite automata for translating the binary strings to turtle drawing instructions. The use of finite automata allows the same binary string to produce many different drawings. We also used finite automata and a context free language generator to exhaustively look at L-system strings of a specified form of lengths 4 through 6.

The first part of this book covers Christoffel words, automatic sequences, and paper folding. A testament to the richness of Christoffel words is the fact that it occupies nearly half the book. The second part of the book covers Lindenmayer systems. Appendix A lists the automaton files used in the book, which can also be downloaded from the book's website. Appendix B is a table of continued fractions for square roots from 2 to 99, useful for Christoffel words. Appendix C describes the software we have developed for this book. And finally there is a reading list for going further.

May you find beautiful patterns in the infinite world of computational images.

Stefan Hollos and Richard Hollos
Exstrom Laboratories LLC
Longmont, Colorado
Nov 18, 2013

INTRODUCTION

A mathematician, like a painter or a poet, is a maker of patterns. If his patterns are more permanent than theirs, it is because they are made with ideas.

G. H. Hardy, A Mathematician's Apology

Humans seem to have an affinity for patterns. Interesting patterns have the ability to capture and hold our attention like nothing else. The structure of music, poetry, painting, sculpture, and almost any art form you can think of is based on patterns.

But what exactly are patterns and where do they come from? Many of them can be found in nature. Plants, animals and inanimate matter exhibit an infinite variety of shapes, patterns and symmetries. The leaves and flowers on a plant, the bark on a tree, spots on a leopard, stripes on a zebra, plumage of a peacock, clouds in the sky, snowflakes, ripples in a stream, are just a few examples.

Since natural patterns are the result of physical laws at work, it suggests that a mathematical approach to their description should be possible. Mathematics has indeed been described, in recent times, as the science of patterns. In our opinion, mathematics is itself an inexhaustible art form, so that using it to describe patterns, the structural basis of all art, seems only natural.

Mathematics is most powerful when it deals with abstractions and generalities. The simplest abstract model of a pattern is a string of symbols. In particular consider binary strings composed of only the symbols 0 and 1. The uniform string composed of all 0's or all 1's is the ultimate in dullness. The string of alternating 0's and 1's is hardly less dull. More complicated repetitive strings start to become more interesting but the really interesting strings are the ones with some non repetitive structure. These are the strings we are interested in.

The first part of the book looks at ways to mathematically create such strings and then interpret them to create interesting geometrical patterns. We start by looking at Christoffel words which are binary words derived from the properties of numbers. We then look at using what are called automatic sequences to create binary strings. Finally we look at paper folding as a way to generate binary strings.

Once we have a binary string, it needs to be translated into drawing instructions to create a visual pattern. We show a very general way of doing this using what we call a translation automaton. This is a finite automaton where every state has a drawing instruction associated with it. What a finite automaton is and how to use it is explained in the book.

The second part of the book is based on the biologically inspired idea of L-systems. Biologists from Aristotle to the present day, have used similarities in the structure of plants and animals to group and classify them. The recognition of these similarities naturally led biologists to the question of whether or not there exist general rules governing how certain patterns and structures develop. The search for an answer to this question led a mathematical biologist named Aristid Lindenmayer to develop a system for modeling plant development now called L-system theory.

L-system theory uses a small set of simple rules to generate a string of symbols. When these symbols are properly interpreted they can be used to create a graphical representation of a plant. A comparison with DNA is irresistible even if not completely justified. DNA can also be thought to be composed of a string of symbols; the symbols being the four bases adenine, thymine, cytosine and guanine.

L-systems are also good at representing objects called fractals. Fractals are objects which have the property of being composed of copies of themselves i.e. a part of a fractal object is a small scale copy of the whole object. This property is called self similarity and is also shared by plants. Some of the best examples of self similar plants are ferns such as Bracken and Lady Fern.

This part of the book will present an introduction to L-systems and show you what you can create with them. We will start with a formal definition of L-systems. An understanding of the formal definition is not necessary for using them to generate plants and patterns. The formal definition is followed by a description of the graphical interpretation of L-systems. An understanding of the graphical interpretation is essential in order to design new plants

Figure 1: A fern shows self similarity.

and patterns. The remainder of the book describes different types of L-systems with numerous examples.

Words, Sequences and Folding

CHRISTOFFEL WORDS

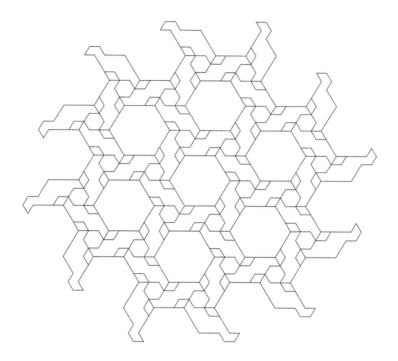

Some of the simplest nontrivial binary patterns are known as Christoffel words. Despite their simplicity they can be used to produce intricate visual patterns. One of the patterns is shown above and there are many more on the following pages. The number of patterns you can create using Christoffel words is infinite. Before describing the algorithms used to generate these patterns we should look at what exactly Christoffel words are and how to construct them.

Figure 2: Elwin Bruno Christoffel (1829-1900). Photo credit: wikipedia.org

Christoffel words are named after *Elwin Bruno Christoffel* (1829-1900), a German mathematician and physicist. They originated in the study of continued fractions and have since found uses in other areas of mathematics. They are part of the study of the combinatorics of words. In mathematics a word is simply a string of symbols chosen from an alphabet. Christoffel words can be constructed from any binary alphabet (an alphabet of only two symbols) but we will stick to using the numbers 0 and 1. For an excellent summary of the mathematics of Christoffel words see reference Berstel et al.. We're going to keep the mathematics to the minimum necessary to understand how Christoffel words (C-words) are constructed.

The simplest geometric method for constructing C-words uses a grid of equally spaced horizontal and vertical lines like in figure 3. In mathematics this is called a Cartesian grid. Vertical lines are numbered left to right starting with zero. Horizontal lines are numbered bottom to top starting with zero. The point where a vertical and horizontal line intersect is labeled by the respective line numbers. Three of these intersection points, $(5, 4)$, $(3, 1)$, and $(6, 2)$ are labeled in the figure.

Every intersection point has a Christoffel word associated with it. As an example let's construct the word for point $(5, 4)$. Start by drawing a line from $(0, 0)$ to $(5, 4)$ as shown in the figure. As you move along the line from $(0, 0)$ to $(5, 4)$ it will intersect a series of vertical and horizontal lines. Label each vertical line intersection with a 0 and each horizontal line intersection with a 1. Now if you label the starting point 0 and the ending point 1 then the sequence of 0's and 1's is 001010101 which is the Christoffel word for $(5, 4)$.

An equivalent construction is to move from point $(0, 0)$ to $(5, 4)$ using only horizontal and vertical steps along grid lines, staying as close as possible below the line from $(0, 0)$ to $(5, 4)$ without crossing it. If horizontal steps are labeled 0 and vertical steps are labeled 1 then the path is

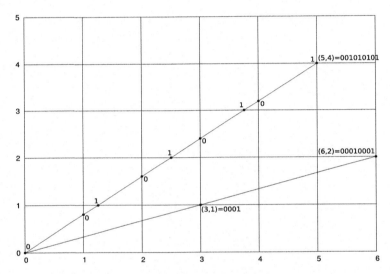

Figure 3: Constructing Christoffel Words.

the Christoffel word 001010101 for $(5,4)$ as in the above construction.

You can construct a Christoffel word for any point on the grid and each word will be unique. No two points have the same word. However, the word for some points will be repetitions of the word for another point.[1] For example $(6,2) = 00010001$, which is two repetitions of the word $(3,1) = 0001$. Notice in this case that $(6,2) = (2 \cdot 3, 2 \cdot 1) = 2 \cdot (3,1)$ so $(6,2)$ is a multiple of 2 times $(3,1)$.

If a generic point (x,y) is a multiple n of another point, so that $(x,y) = (n \cdot a, n \cdot b) = n \cdot (a,b)$ then the word for (x,y) will be composed of n copies of the word for (a,b). To avoid words with repetitions you want to pick a point (x,y) where the numbers x and y have no common factors i.e. you cannot write x and y as $x = n \cdot a$ and $y = n \cdot b$ for some integers a, b, and n.

Another way to look at the construction of C-words is in terms of the slope of a line. A line from $(0,0)$ to point (x,y) will have a slope of y/x. The slope is essentially the steepness of the line. It is the ratio of how far you move in the vertical direction for a given amount of movement in the horizontal direction while traveling along the line. The larger the slope the steeper the line. If point A is a multiple of point B then the line from $(0,0)$ to A has the same slope as the line from $(0,0)$ to B so they are really the same lines and the Christoffel word for A is a repeat

---

[1]A word that is a repetition of another word is not, strictly speaking, a Christoffel word, but for our purposes we will treat it as one.

of the word for B. You can see this for $A = (6, 2)$ and $B = (3, 1)$ in figure 3.

We will stick to associating Christoffel words with the slope, y/x of a line starting from the origin. The assumption will be that both y and x are integers so that the slope is a rational number. If the slope were an irrational number such as $\sqrt{2}$ then the line would never intersect another lattice point and the Christoffel word would be infinitely long. It would become what the mathematicians call a *Sturmian sequence*. You can always get as close as you want to an irrational slope by using a rational approximation. We will show how to do this in some of the following examples.

One more way to construct Christoffel words is by using the trajectory of a billiard ball on a square billiard table. You launch a billiard ball from the lower left corner of the table in the direction of a line with slope y/x. The ball will bounce off the sides of the table and eventually end up in one of the corners after $x + y - 2$ bounces. An example is shown in figure 4 for $y/x = 4/5$.

If you label the start with a 0, a bounce off a vertical side with a 0, a bounce off a horizontal side with a 1, and the end with a 1, then the trajectory defines the Christoffel word for slope y/x. This method can obviously be generalized to trajectories inside shapes other than squares.

Luckily you don't have to manually construct Christoffel words using any of the methods discussed so far. There's a simple algorithm that will generate the word for you. To create the word for y/x start by creating two lists of numbers: $L_0 = [y, 2y, 3y, \ldots, (x-1)y]$ and $L_1 = [x, 2x, 3x, \ldots, (y-$

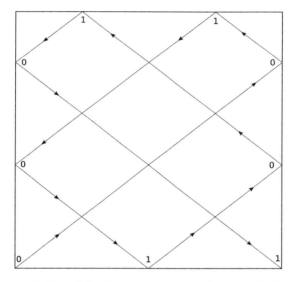

Figure 4: Billiard ball trajectory with initial slope 4/5.

1)x]. Next combine the two lists into a single sorted list. Examine each element of the sorted list. If it comes from L_0 replace it with a 0 and if it comes from L_1 replace it with a 1. Now add a 0 to the beginning and a 1 to the end of the list and you have the Christoffel word for y/x. Actually implementing the algorithm is much simpler than it sounds since the creation of the sorted list and conversion to 0's and 1's can be done in a single step. The algorithm in pseudo code is shown below (note that a != b means a not equal to b).

```
a = y
b = x
print 0
while( a != b )
{
  if( a > b )
  {
    print 1
    b = b + x
  }
  else
  {
    print 0
    a = a + y
  }
}
print 1
```

The program chseq will calculate the C-word for any slope y/x. Run it as:

```
chseq y x
```
and it will print the C-word. This program, as well as all the other programs used in this book, are written in the C programming language. There is a C language compiler for every major operating system. A good one that is also free is *gcc*.

From the above algorithm it is clear that you can get the C-word for x/y simply by exchanging the 0's and 1's in the C-word for y/x. Also the length of the C-word for y/x will always equal $y + x$. One more thing to note is that if you remove the 0 at the beginning and the 1 at the end of a C-word then what you are left with is a palindrome, which is a word that reads the same both forward and backward. This may be useful to know when deciding how to turn a C-word into a drawing which is what we will discuss next.

Drawing Translation

A Christoffel word is just a string of 0's and 1's. To turn it into a drawing it needs to be translated into drawing instructions. A very general way to do this is to use a finite automaton. This is much simpler than it sounds. An example of a finite automaton is shown in the figure below.

The automaton is a translation machine. Circled numbers represent states, and the arrows represent transitions between states. It starts in state 0, and as you feed it a sequence of binary numbers, it transitions to other states. Each state has an output associated with it. When the

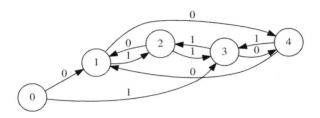

Figure 5: 1-bit parity automaton

machine enters a particular state, it prints the output associated with that state. In our case, the outputs will be drawing instructions. To keep things simple, we will limit the drawing instructions to the letters +, -, F, f. These are turtle graphics commands that will be interpreted by a turtle graphics program to produce an image.

As an example, for the above automaton we could make the outputs F, +F, -F, and F for states 1, 2, 3, and 4 respectively. Note that state 0, the start state, never has an output associated with it. So if we feed this automaton 00100101 which is the C-word for 3/5 it will start in state 0 and then go to state 1 and output an F when it reads the first 0. When it reads the second 0, it goes to state 4 and outputs another F. When it reads the first 1, it goes to state 3 and outputs -F. This continues on until the entire input is read, resulting in the final output of $FF - FFF + FF + F$.

This particular automaton was designed to differentiate

whether a 0 or 1 is at an even or odd position. A 0 at an even position puts the automaton in state 1 and a 0 at an odd position puts it in state 4. A 1 at an even position puts the automaton in state 3 and a 1 at an odd position puts it in state 2.

You can create a translation automaton with any number of states. The only requirement is that each state have two transitions one for reading 0 and one for reading 1. State 0 is always the start state and it only has transitions going out. The output for a state can be any string of drawing instructions, or it can be an empty string. The following are examples of some other automatons that we used to translate C-words into drawing instructions.

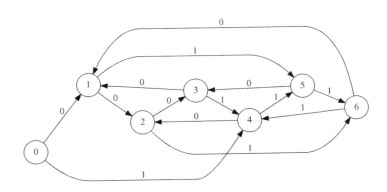

Figure 6: 1-bit 3-positions automaton

The automaton in figure 6 was designed to differentiate if a 0 or 1 is at a position number whose remainder after dividing by 3 is 0, 1 or 2. Call these positions (0 mod 3), (1 mod 3), and (2 mod 3). States $1 - 3$ correspond to 0's at (0 mod 3), (1 mod 3), and (2 mod 3) respectively. States $4 - 6$ correspond to 1's at (0 mod 3), (1 mod 3), and (2 mod 3) respectively. For example if there's a 1 at position 5 then the automaton will be in state 6 since 5 leaves a remainder of 2 after division by 3 so the position is (2 mod 3).

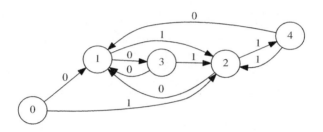

Figure 7: Count run lengths up to 2 automaton

The automaton in figure 7 was designed to count runs up to length 2. For example, after reading the first 0, we have a 0 run of length 1. If the next number is also a 0, then we have a run of length 2. If the next number is again a 0, then the run count resets to 1. State 1 corresponds to a 0 with run count 1. State 2 corresponds to a 1 with run count 1. State 3 to a 0 with run count 2, and state 4 to a 1 with run count 2.

The automaton in figure 8 is the same as the previous,

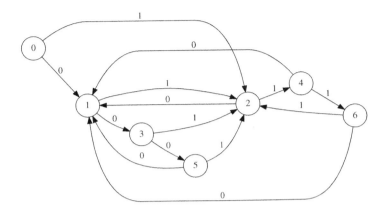

Figure 8: Count run lengths up to 3 automaton

except that it counts runs up to length 3.

The automata in figures 9, 10 and 11 are based on de Bruijn graphs. You can simply use them as they are. The theory behind them can be found on *Wikipedia*.

You can use these automata to translate any binary string with the program `katrans` that can be downloaded from the book's web page. The program reads an automaton file that defines the automaton used for the translation. For example, the automaton file for figure 9 is

```
; 2-bit de Bruijn graph
7 2
0 1 2
```

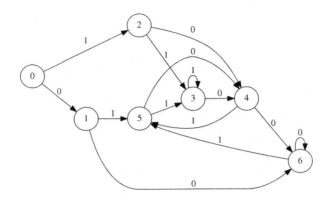

Figure 9: 2-bit de Bruijn graph automaton

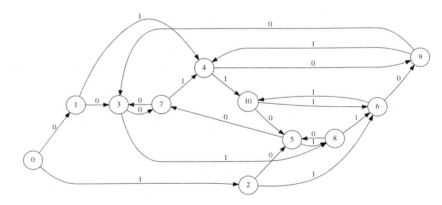

Figure 10: 2-bit de Bruijn graph with parity split automaton

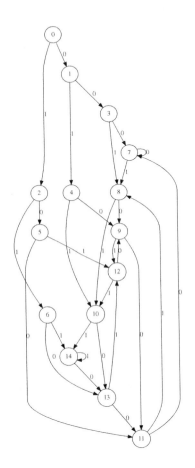

Figure 11: 3-bit de Bruijn graph automaton

```
1 6 5
2 4 3
3 4 3 +F
4 6 5 -F
5 4 3 -F
6 6 5 +F
```

The first line that begins with a semicolon is a comment. The second line has the number of states (7) and the number of transitions out of each state (2). Each line after that defines one of the states. The first number on the line is the state number. The next number is the state to transition to when a 0 is read. The last number is the state to transition to when a 1 is read. After the numbers comes the drawing instruction that is output when that state is entered. Note in this case that only states 3 through 6 have outputs. You can enter any string that you like for drawing instructions. This is where you can experiment to produce different drawings for a given C-word and translation automaton.

Producing a Drawing

Now we will describe the entire process of producing a drawing. First choose a rational number y/x. Then run the program chseq which can also be downloaded from this book's web page. The program, like all the programs in this book, are console programs that are run on the command line. chseq takes three inputs: y, x, and n, where n

is the number of terms of the Christoffel word for y/x that the program should print out. If n is greater than $y + x$ then it will just repeat the C-word. For most of the drawings in this book you will want n to be some multiple of $y + x$. The output of chseq can either be put into a file or directly sent to the program katrans which, as described above, will translate it into drawing instructions using an automaton. katrans takes only one input, the name of the automaton file. The output of katrans can either be put into a file or fed directly into the turtle graphics drawing program called turtledraw. The program turtledraw produces an SVG file. It takes three inputs: a start angle, a turn angle, and the name of the SVG file that you want it to produce. The input string is read from standard input. The following is an example of a single command line that can be used to produce a drawing:

```
chseq 355 113 1872 | katrans t7.kat | turtledraw 0.0 90.0 out.svg
```

giving us the SVG file out.svg which can be viewed in a web browser like Firefox, or a graphics program like display from *Imagemagick*, or a vector graphics editing program like Inkscape. The resulting image is shown below.

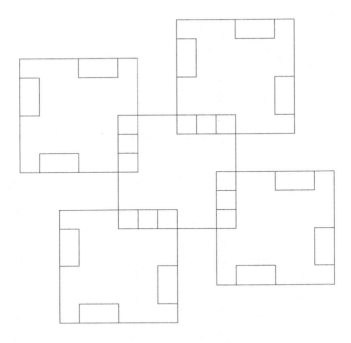

The file **t7.kat** used to produce the above image, as well as other .kat files used to make the figures on the following pages are listed in the appendix and can also be found on this book's web page. Following are more images produced as above, and preceded by the command line that produced them.

chseq 11 12 500 | katrans t1.kat | turtledraw 0.0 170.0 out.svg

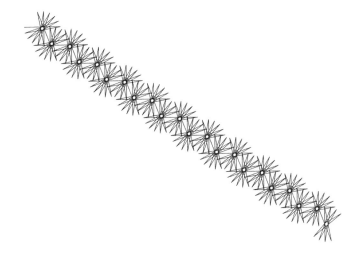

chseq 11 12 500 | katrans t1.kat | turtledraw 0.0 179.0 out.svg

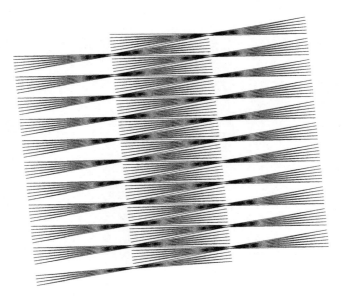

chseq 5 7 108 | katrans t1.kat | turtledraw 0.0 160.0 out.svg

chseq 6 7 500 | katrans t1.kat | turtledraw 0.0 45.0 out.svg

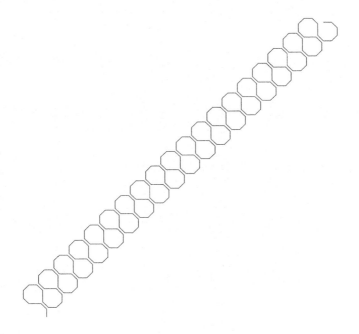

chseq 6 7 500 | katrans t1.kat | turtledraw 0.0 55.0 out.svg

chseq 9 10 684 | katrans t5.kat | turtledraw 0.0 170.0 out.svg

chseq 9 10 76 | katrans t6.kat | turtledraw 0.0 170.0 out.svg

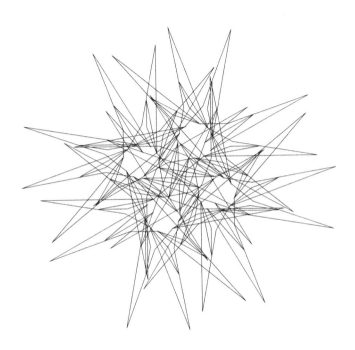

chseq 9 10 684 | katrans t7.kat | turtledraw 0.0 170.0 out.svg

chseq 9 10 171 | katrans t10.kat | turtledraw 0.0 170.0 out.svg

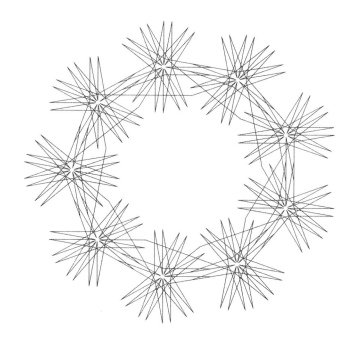

chseq 11 12 414 | katrans t10.kat | turtledraw 0.0 170.0 out.svg

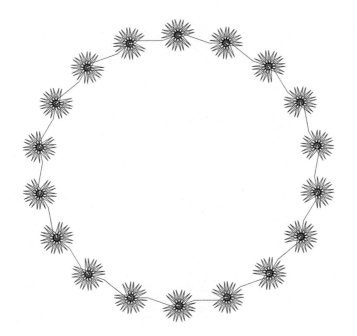

chseq 5 7 432 | katrans t1.kat | turtledraw 0.0 170.0 out.svg

chseq 5 7 432 | katrans t10.kat | turtledraw 0.0 170.0 out.svg

chseq 13 17 1080 | katrans t6.kat | turtledraw 0.0 170.0 out.svg

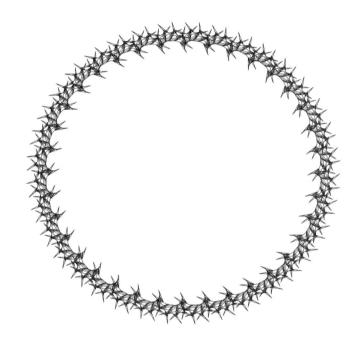

chseq 7 5 864 | katrans t1.kat | turtledraw 0.0 175.0 out.svg

chseq 7 5 432 | katrans t1.kat | turtledraw 0.0 150.0 out.svg

chseq 41 29 420 | katrans t15.kat | turtledraw 0.0 175.0 out.svg

`chseq 169 99 1608 | katrans t1.kat | turtledraw 0.0 60.0 out.svg`

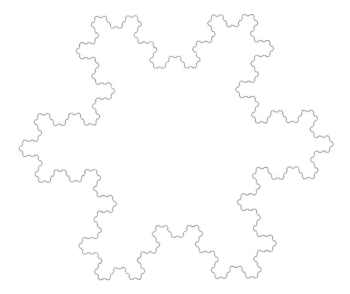

`chseq 169 99 804 | katrans t3.kat | turtledraw 0.0 60.0 out.svg`

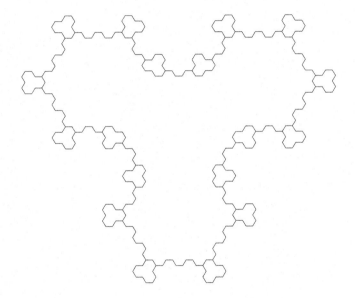

49

chseq 169 99 804 | katrans t4.kat | turtledraw 0.0 30.0 out.svg

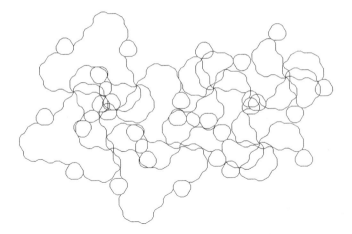

`chseq 193 71 3168 | katrans t12.kat | turtledraw 0.0 30.0 out.svg`

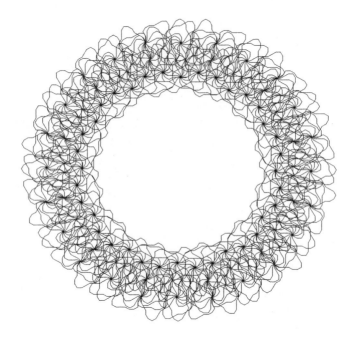

chseq 193 71 1056 | katrans t1.kat | turtledraw 0.0 90.0 out.svg

chseq 193 71 1056 | katrans t7.kat | turtledraw 0.0 90.0 out.svg

chseq 193 71 1584 | katrans t1.kat | turtledraw 0.0 60.0 out.svg

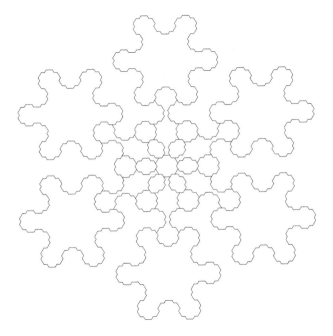

chseq 193 71 792 | katrans t2.kat | turtledraw 0.0 60.0 out.svg

chseq 193 71 1914 | katrans t5.kat | turtledraw 0.0 170.0 out.svg

chseq 193 71 528 | katrans t3.kat | turtledraw 0.0 15.0 out.svg

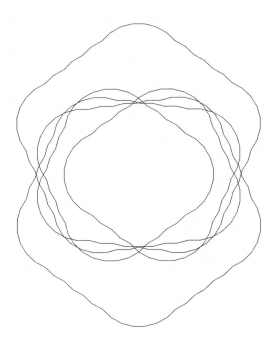

chseq 21 13 136 | katrans t10.kat | turtledraw 0.0 90.0 out.svg

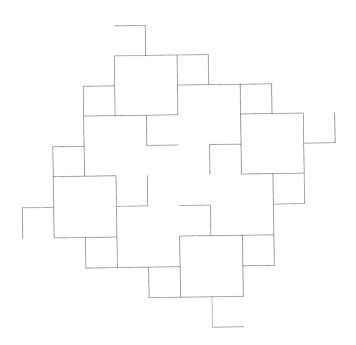

`chseq 377 233 2440 | katrans t9.kat | turtledraw 0.0 90.0 out.svg`

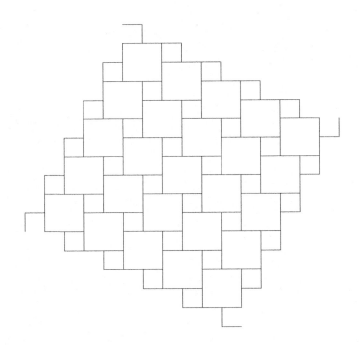

chseq 1597 987 10336 | katrans t1.kat | turtledraw 0.0 90.0 out.svg

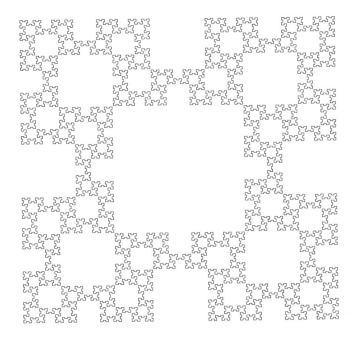

```
chseq 377 233 2440 | katrans t1.kat | turtledraw 0.0 120.0 out.svg
```

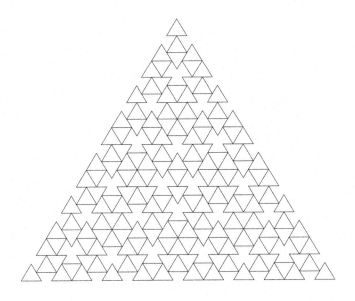

chseq 89 55 1296 | katrans t1.kat | turtledraw 0.0 160.0 out.svg

chseq 5 3 72 | katrans t13.kat | turtledraw 0.0 160.0 out.svg

chseq 21 13 1224 | katrans t1.kat | turtledraw 0.0 170.0 out.svg

Continued Fractions

The program chseq will only produce Christoffel words for rational numbers. The Christoffel word for an irrational number is infinitely long and is called a Sturmian sequence. It is possible however to use chseq to look at Christoffel words for the rational approximations of an irrational number. Take the square root of 2 as an example, its value to 20 decimal places is $\sqrt{2} = 1.41421356237309504880\ldots$. A table of $\sqrt{2}$ along with some increasingly accurate rational approximations is shown below.

$\sqrt{2}$	$1.414213562373095\ldots$
$\frac{7}{5}$	1.4
$\frac{17}{12}$	1.41666666666666
$\frac{41}{29}$	1.41379310344827
$\frac{99}{70}$	1.41428571428571
$\frac{239}{169}$	1.41420118343195
$\frac{577}{408}$	1.41421568627451

These rational approximations come from the continued fraction for $\sqrt{2}$. A continued fraction is like a regular fraction except that the denominator also contains a fraction, and that fraction's denominator also contains a fraction, and so on. A simple continued fraction looks like the following

$$a_0 + \cfrac{1}{a_1 + \cfrac{1}{a_2 + \cfrac{1}{a_3 + \cfrac{1}{a_4 + \cdots}}}}$$

This is usually abbreviated by just listing the numbers like so: $[a_0, a_1, a_2, a_3 \ldots]$. Both rational and irrational numbers have continued fractions. For a rational number, the continued fraction ends at some point, while for an irrational number, it continues on forever. The square root of an integer that is not a perfect square is irrational and its continued fraction goes on forever, but at some point it begins to repeat. The continued fraction for $\sqrt{n}$ will look like $[a_0, \overline{a_1, a_2, \ldots, a_k}]$ where the bar over the terms following a_0 indicate that they repeat forever. So if $k = 2$ the continued fraction would be $[a_0, a_1, a_2, a_1, a_2, \ldots]$. Two interesting facts about these square root continued fractions is that the a_k term will always be twice the a_0 term, and if you remove the a_k term, the remaining terms in the repeating part form a palindrome.

As an example, let's first look at the continued fraction for a rational number like 7/5. Start by writing

$$\frac{7}{5} = 1 + \frac{2}{5} = 1 + \frac{1}{\frac{5}{2}} = 1 + \frac{1}{2 + \frac{1}{2}}$$

So writing this in list form, we have $7/5 = [1, 2, 2]$. The same basic thing can be done for an irrational number like $\sqrt{2}$. This gives

$$\sqrt{2} = 1 + \cfrac{1}{2 + \cfrac{1}{2 + \cfrac{1}{2 + \cfrac{1}{2 + \cdots}}}}$$

Here the continued fraction goes on forever with the 2 repeating, which we write as $\sqrt{2} = [1, \overline{2}]$. The bar over the 2 signifies that the 2 repeats forever. Note that the $7/5$ example that we worked out contains the first 3 terms of the continued fraction for $\sqrt{2}$ and that $7/5$ is one of the rational approximations that we listed above for $\sqrt{2}$. In general to get a rational approximation for a square root, you use a finite number of the beginning terms of its continued fraction. So the next rational approximation for $\sqrt{2}$ is $17/12 = [1, 2, 2, 2]$ and so on.

These increasingly accurate rational approximations are called convergents. Using the convergents of $\sqrt{2}$ with chseq, then feeding the result into katrans with the automata listed in the appendix, and finally using turtledraw with various turn angles results in the following images.

chseq 239 169 4896 | katrans t1.kat | turtledraw 0.0 60.0 out.svg

chseq 7 5 120 | katrans t0b.kat | turtledraw 0.0 45.0 out.svg

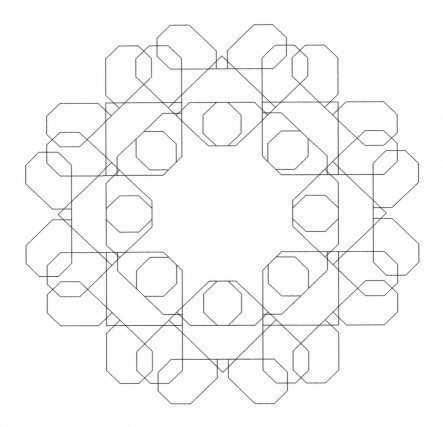

chseq 577 408 985 | katrans t2.kat | turtledraw 0.0 45.0 out.svg

chseq 7 5 120 | katrans t6.kat | turtledraw 0.0 45.0 out.svg

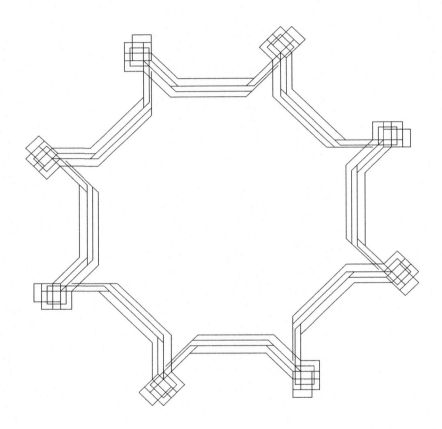

chseq 7 5 120 | katrans t7.kat | turtledraw 0.0 45.0 out.svg

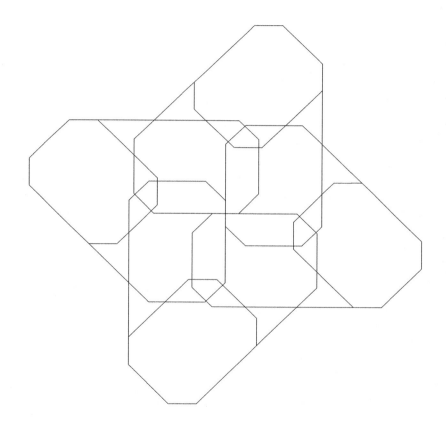

chseq 7 5 120 | katrans t10.kat | turtledraw 0.0 45.0 out.svg

chseq 7 5 120 | katrans t0a.kat | turtledraw 0.0 60.0 out.svg

chseq 577 408 985 | katrans t10.kat | turtledraw 0.0 60.0 out.svg

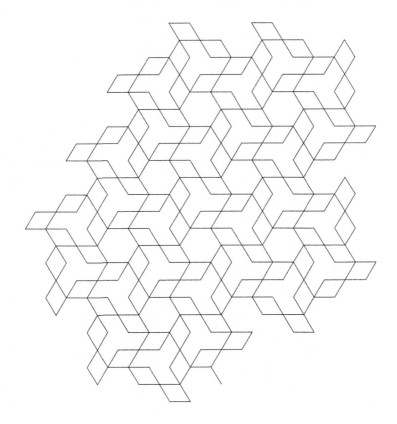

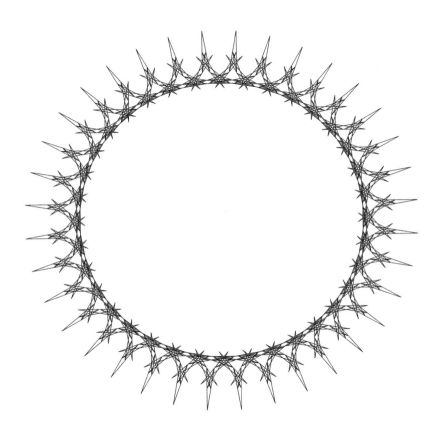

chseq 17 12 1044 | katrans t0.kat | turtledraw 0.0 170.0 out.svg

chseq 41 29 630 | katrans t7.kat | turtledraw 0.0 170.0 out.svg

Square Root of 3

Now let's look at a few other square roots. Appendix B lists continued fractions for square roots of integers less than 100. You can also use the program `cfsqrt` to calculate the continued fraction for the square root of any integer. Run it as

`cfsqrt n`

where `n` is the integer whose square root you want the continued fraction for. Running the program for n= 3 prints out the three numbers 1 1 2 so the continued fraction is $\sqrt{3} = [1, \overline{1, 2}]$. Note that for any square root the numbers following the first number will be the repeating part of the continued fraction. To find the convergents you can run the program `cfcv` with however many terms of the continued fraction you want to use. The more terms, the more accurate the convergent. For $\sqrt{3}$ running

`cfcv 1 1 2`

will output 5 3 which is the convergent 5/3 for the first 3 terms of the continued fraction. To add two more terms run

`cfcv 1 1 2 1 2`

which outputs 19 11 which is the convergent 19/11 for the first 5 terms of the continued fraction. The following table shows the first few convergents for $\sqrt{3}$ along with its actual value to 20 decimal places, $\sqrt{3} = 1.73205080756887729352\ldots$.

$$\sqrt{3} \quad 1.73205080756887729352\ldots$$

$$\frac{5}{3} \quad 1.66666666666666$$

$$\frac{7}{4} \quad 1.75$$

$$\frac{19}{11} \quad 1.727272727272727$$

$$\frac{26}{15} \quad 1.733333333333333$$

$$\frac{71}{41} \quad 1.731707317073171$$

$$\frac{97}{56} \quad 1.732142857142857$$

$$\frac{265}{153} \quad 1.73202614379085$$

Using the convergents of $\sqrt{3}$ with chseq, as was done with $\sqrt{2}$, some of the resulting images are shown on the following pages.

chseq 71 41 896 | katrans t0a.kat | turtledraw 0.0 45.0 out.svg

chseq 19 11 480 | katrans t0b.kat | turtledraw 0.0 45.0 out.svg

chseq 19 11 480 | katrans t2.kat | turtledraw 0.0 45.0 out.svg

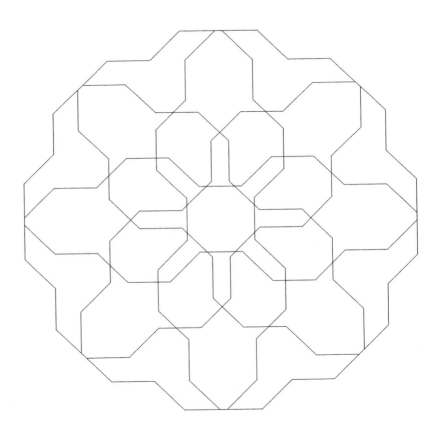

chseq 26 15 656 | katrans t2.kat | turtledraw 0.0 45.0 out.svg

chseq 265 153 3344 | katrans t2.kat | turtledraw 0.0 45.0 out.svg

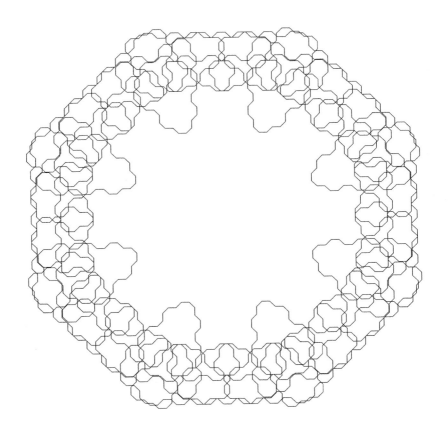

chseq 7 4 176 | katrans t10.kat | turtledraw 0.0 45.0 out.svg

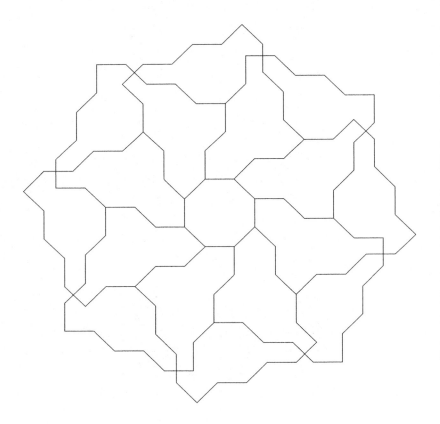

chseq 7 4 176 | katrans t11.kat | turtledraw 0.0 45.0 out.svg

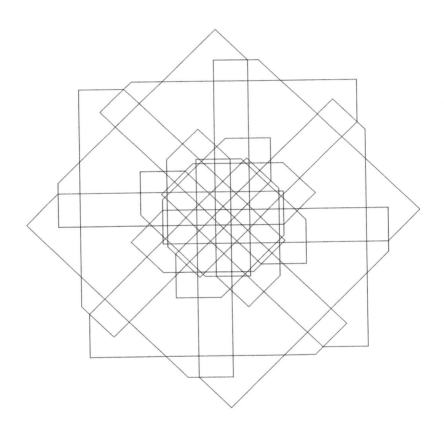

chseq 26 15 656 | katrans t13.kat | turtledraw 0.0 45.0 out.svg

chseq 19 11 480 | katrans t0a.kat | turtledraw 0.0 60.0 out.svg

chseq 19 11 480 | katrans t2.kat | turtledraw 0.0 60.0 out.svg

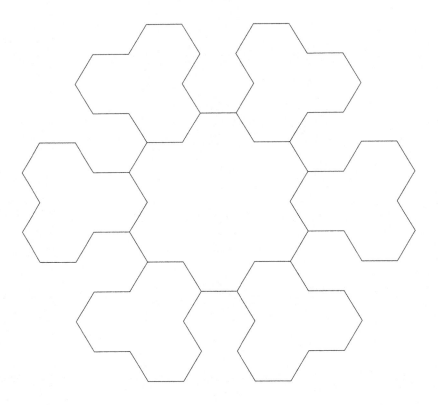

chseq 97 56 1224 | katrans t10.kat | turtledraw 0.0 60.0 out.svg

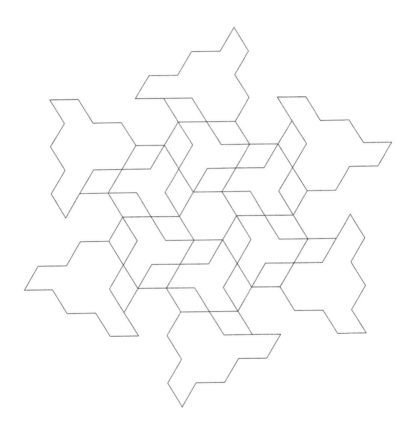

chseq 97 56 1224 | katrans t12.kat | turtledraw 0.0 60.0 out.svg

chseq 19 11 480 | katrans t0a.kat | turtledraw 0.0 90.0 out.svg

chseq 265 153 1672 | katrans t1.kat | turtledraw 0.0 90.0 out.svg

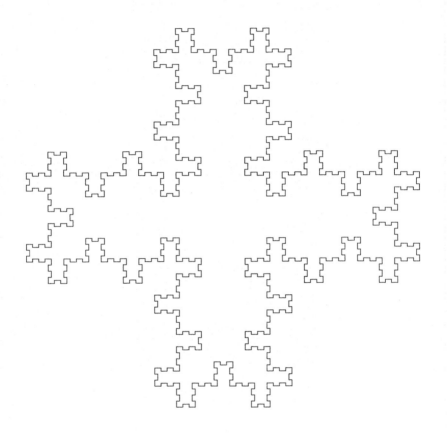

chseq 265 153 1672 | katrans t2.kat | turtledraw 0.0 90.0 out.svg

chseq 19 11 1080 | katrans t0.kat | turtledraw 0.0 170.0 out.svg

chseq 26 15 738 | katrans t10.kat | turtledraw 0.0 170.0 out.svg

chseq 5 3 144 | katrans t13.kat | turtledraw 0.0 170.0 out.svg

chseq 71 41 672 | katrans t15.kat | turtledraw 0.0 170.0 out.svg

Square Root of 5

We will look at a couple more examples using square root convergents before moving on to more general irrational numbers. First let's look at $\sqrt{5}$. The continued fraction is $\sqrt{5} = [2, \overline{4}]$ and the first few convergents, calculated using the program cfcv, are shown in the table below.

$\sqrt{5}$	2.23606797749978969640...
$\frac{9}{4}$	2.25
$\frac{38}{17}$	2.235294117647059
$\frac{161}{72}$	2.236111111111111
$\frac{682}{305}$	2.236065573770492
$\frac{2889}{1292}$	2.236068111455108
$\frac{12238}{5473}$	2.236067970034716
$\frac{51841}{23184}$	2.236067977915804

The following are some of the images you can generate with these convergents.

chseq 9 4 26 | katrans t0b.kat | turtledraw 0.0 45.0 out.svg

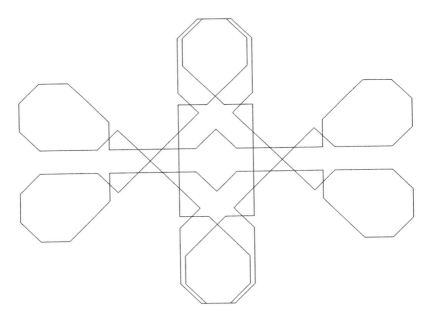

chseq 9 4 52 | katrans t10.kat | turtledraw 0.0 45.0 out.svg

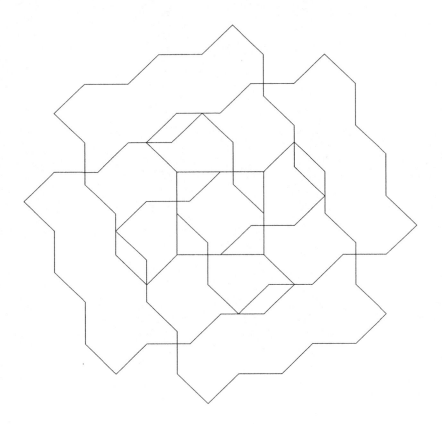

chseq 9 4 104 | katrans t12.kat | turtledraw 0.0 45.0 out.svg

chseq 682 305 1974 | katrans t12.kat | turtledraw 0.0 45.0 out.svg

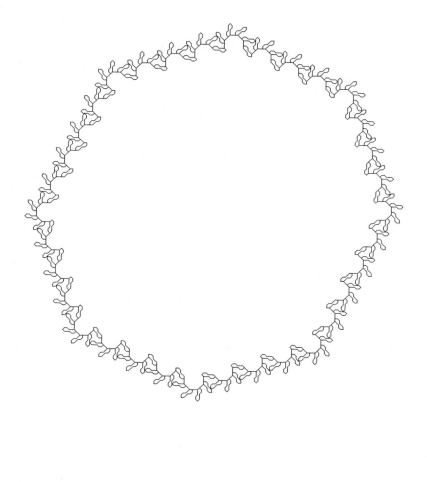

chseq 38 17 220 | katrans t0c.kat | turtledraw 0.0 90.0 out.svg

chseq 682 305 987 | katrans t6.kat | turtledraw 0.0 90.0 out.svg

chseq 38 17 220 | katrans t7.kat | turtledraw 0.0 90.0 out.svg

chseq 682 305 987 | katrans t11.kat | turtledraw 0.0 90.0 out.svg

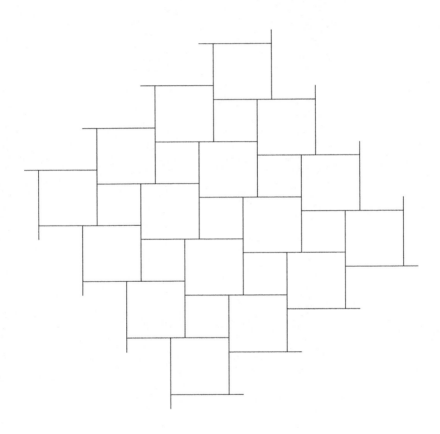

chseq 682 305 987 | katrans t15.kat | turtledraw 0.0 90.0 out.svg

chseq 682 305 17766 | katrans t0.kat | turtledraw 0.0 170.0 out.svg

chseq 38 17 1980 | katrans t11.kat | turtledraw 0.0 170.0 out.svg

```
chseq 682 305 987 | katrans t2.kat | turtledraw -90.0 60.0 out.svg
```

chseq 682 305 987 | katrans t7.kat | turtledraw 0.0 60.0 out.svg

Square Root of 17

As one more example let's look at $\sqrt{17}$. The continued fraction is $\sqrt{17} = [4, \overline{8}]$ and the first few convergents, calculated using the program `cfcv`, are shown in the table below.

$\sqrt{17}$	4.12310562561766054982...
$\frac{33}{8}$	4.12500000000000000000
$\frac{268}{65}$	4.12307692307692307692
$\frac{2177}{528}$	4.12310606060606060606
$\frac{17684}{4289}$	4.12310561902541384938
$\frac{143649}{34840}$	4.12310562571756601607
$\frac{1166876}{283009}$	4.12310562561614648297
$\frac{9478657}{2298912}$	4.12310562561768349549

The following are some of the images you can generate with these convergents.

chseq 2177 528 2705 | katrans t0a.kat | turtledraw 0.0 45.0 out.svg

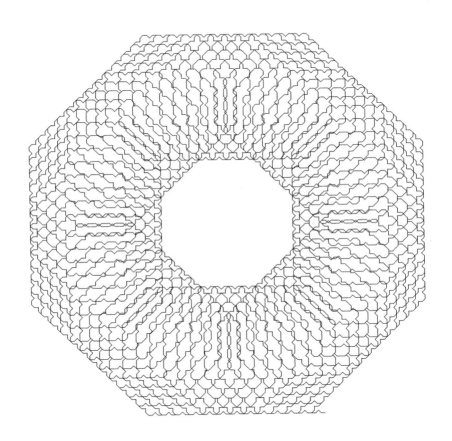

chseq 33 8 164 | katrans t10.kat | turtledraw 0.0 45.0 out.svg

chseq 268 65 333 | katrans t11.kat | turtledraw 0.0 45.0 out.svg

chseq 2177 528 2705 | katrans t13.kat | turtledraw 0.0 45.0 out.svg

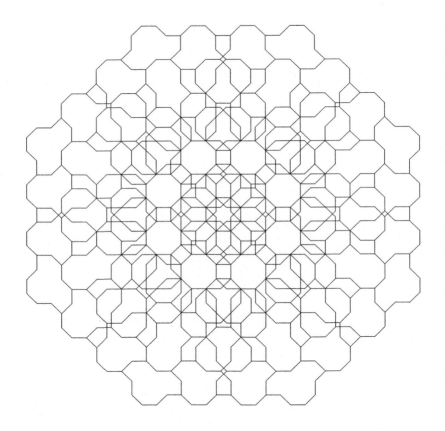

chseq 2177 528 2705 | katrans t15.kat | turtledraw 0.0 45.0 out.svg

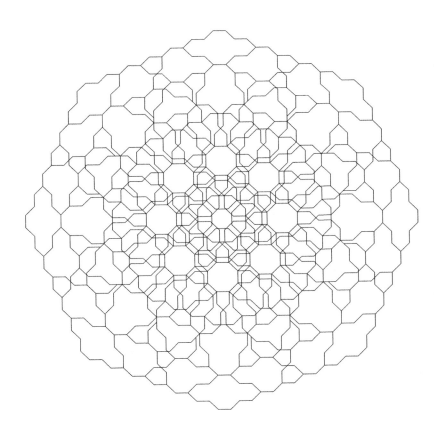

chseq 2177 528 2705 | katrans t4.kat | turtledraw 0.0 60.0 out.svg

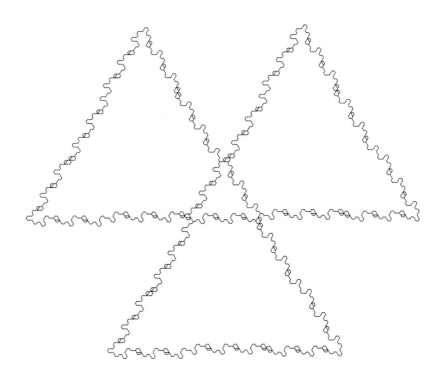

chseq 2177 528 2705 | katrans t15.kat | turtledraw 0.0 60.0 out.svg

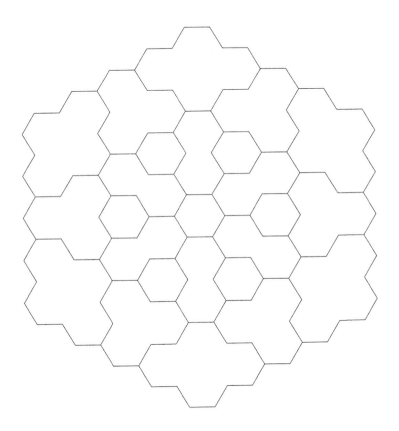

chseq 2177 528 2705 | katrans t0a.kat | turtledraw 0.0 90.0 out.svg

chseq 2177 528 2705 | katrans t6.kat | turtledraw 32.0 90.0 out.svg

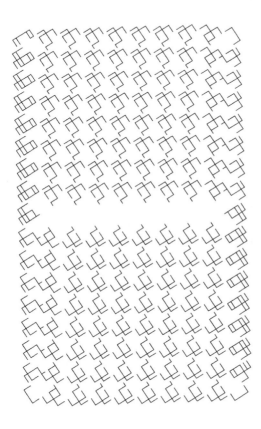

chseq 268 65 2997 | katrans t0.kat | turtledraw 0.0 170.0 out.svg

chseq 33 8 164 | katrans t5.kat | turtledraw 0.0 170.0 out.svg

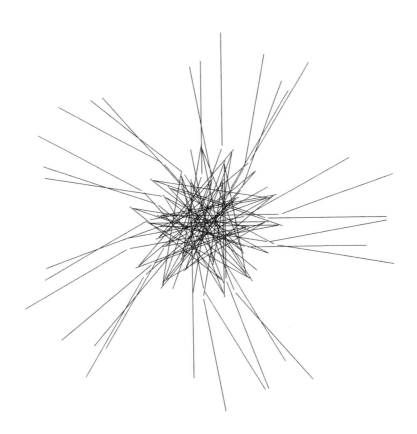

chseq 2177 528 2705 | katrans t7.kat | turtledraw 0.0 170.0 out.svg

Golden Ratio

Now we look at some more general irrational numbers. The simplest of these are the quadratic irrationals. The name comes from the fact that they are roots of quadratic equations with integer coefficients. These are equations of the form: $ax^2 + bx + c = 0$ where a, b, c are integers. The two solutions (roots) of this equation can be written as: $\frac{-b \pm \sqrt{b^2 - 4ac}}{2a}$. If the argument inside the square root is positive, meaning $b^2 > 4ac$ then the roots will be quadratic irrationals with periodic continued fractions like the simple square roots[2].

The quadratic irrational with the simplest continued fraction is the golden ratio: $\phi = \frac{1 + \sqrt{5}}{2}$ which is the positive root of the quadratic equation $x^2 - x - 1 = 0$. The continued fraction is purely periodic: $\phi = [\overline{1}]$, i.e. all of the infinite number of terms are equal to 1. Some of the first few convergents of ϕ are shown in the table below. Following are some images you can generate using these convergents.

---

[2]Simple square roots are, strictly speaking, also quadratic irrationals with $b = 0$, $a = 1$, and $c < 0$, but we are interested here in the more general case.

$\frac{1+\sqrt{5}}{2}$	1.61803398874989484820...
$\frac{5}{3}$	1.66666666666666666666
$\frac{8}{5}$	1.60000000000000000000
$\frac{13}{8}$	1.62500000000000000000
$\frac{21}{13}$	1.61538461538461538461
$\frac{34}{21}$	1.61904761904761904761
$\frac{55}{34}$	1.61764705882352941176
$\frac{89}{55}$	1.61818181818181818181
$\frac{144}{89}$	1.61797752808988764044
$\frac{233}{144}$	1.61805555555555555555
$\frac{377}{233}$	1.61802575107296137339
$\frac{610}{377}$	1.61803713527851458885
$\frac{987}{610}$	1.61803278688524590163
$\frac{1597}{987}$	1.61803444782168186423

chseq 8 5 104 | katrans t0b.kat | turtledraw 0.0 45.0 out.svg

chseq 21 13 272 | katrans t0b.kat | turtledraw 0.0 45.0 out.svg

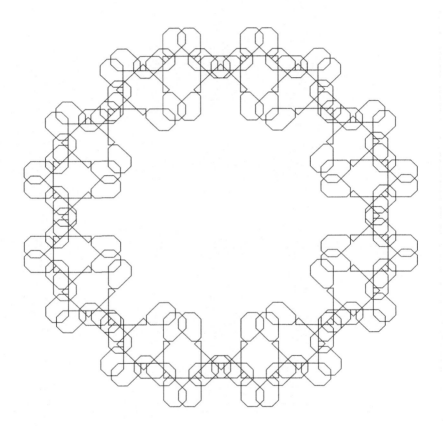

chseq 21 13 272 | katrans t2.kat | turtledraw 0.0 45.0 out.svg

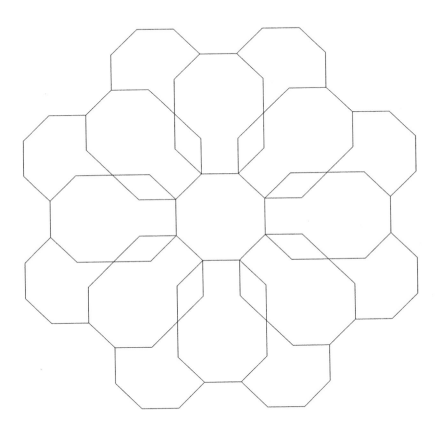

```
chseq 8 5 156 | katrans t4.kat | turtledraw 0.0 45.0 out.svg
```

chseq 8 5 104 | katrans t7.kat | turtledraw 0.0 45.0 out.svg

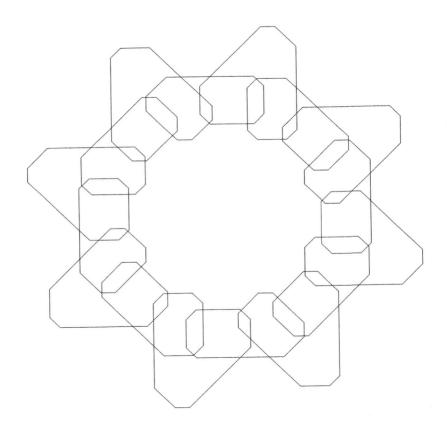

chseq 8 5 117 | katrans t13.kat | turtledraw 0.0 45.0 out.svg

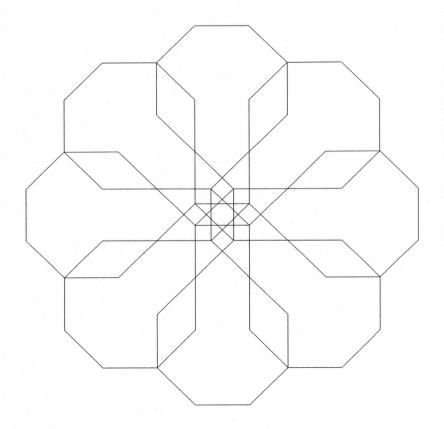

chseq 13 8 168 | katrans t13.kat | turtledraw 0.0 45.0 out.svg

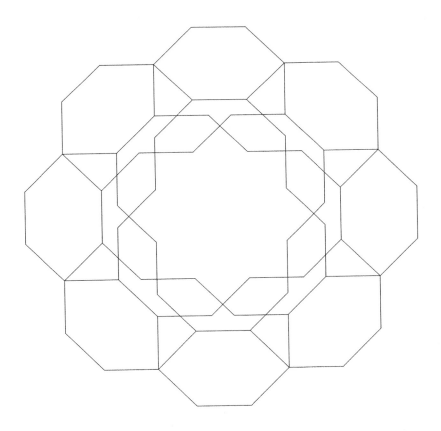

chseq 21 13 136 | katrans t13.kat | turtledraw 0.0 45.0 out.svg

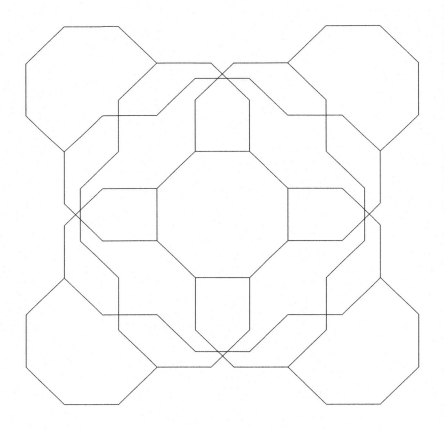

chseq 21 13 204 | katrans t2.kat | turtledraw 0.0 60.0 out.svg

chseq 8 5 117 | katrans t0.kat | turtledraw 0.0 170.0 out.svg

chseq 13 8 84 | katrans t7.kat | turtledraw 0.0 170.0 out.svg

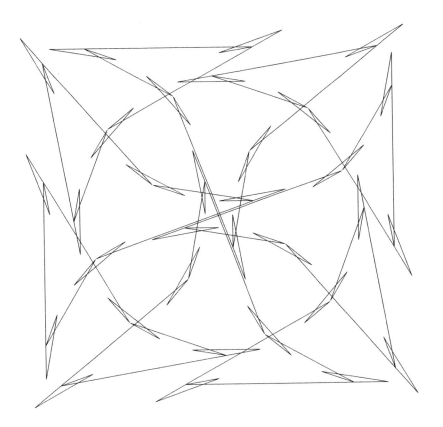

chseq 8 5 468 | katrans t11.kat | turtledraw 0.0 170.0 out.svg

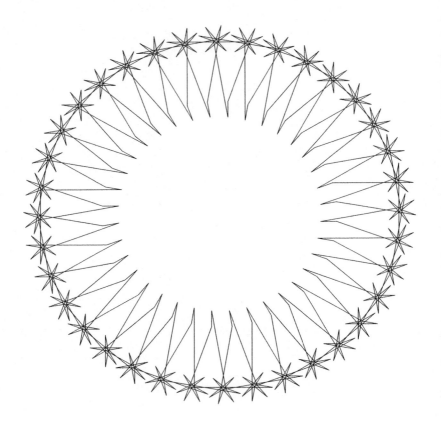

Transcendental Numbers

Another class of irrational numbers are called the transcendental numbers. These numbers are not the roots of any polynomial equation with integer coefficients. Probably the most familiar transcendental number is Pi which is the ratio of a circle's circumference to its diameter and is usually symbolized as π. Its value to 20 decimal places is $\pi = 3.14159265358979323844\ldots$ The continued fraction for π not only goes on forever, but it does not repeat and there is no recognizable pattern to the terms. The first few terms of the continued fraction are
$\pi = [3, 7, 15, 1, 292, 1, 1, 1, 2, 1, 3, 1, 14, \ldots]$.
The first few convergents of π are shown in the table below followed by some images you can generate by using them.

π	$3.14159265358979323844\ldots$
$\frac{22}{7}$	3.14285714285714285714
$\frac{333}{106}$	3.14150943396226415094
$\frac{355}{113}$	3.14159292035398230088
$\frac{103993}{33102}$	3.14159265301190260407
$\frac{104348}{33215}$	3.14159265392142104470

chseq 22 7 174 | katrans t8.kat | turtledraw 0.0 170.0 out.svg

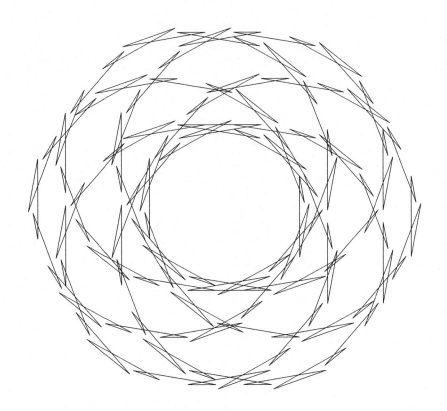

chseq 22 7 116 | katrans t10.kat | turtledraw 0.0 170.0 out.svg

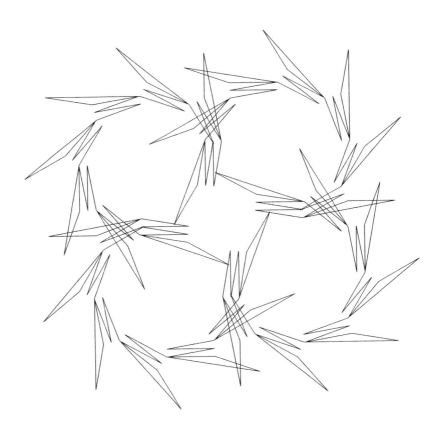

chseq 333 106 2634 | katrans t5.kat | turtledraw 0.0 170.0 out.svg

chseq 355 113 2340 | katrans t4.kat | turtledraw 0.0 15.0 out.svg

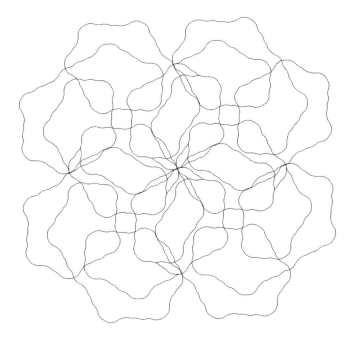

chseq 355 113 2808 | katrans t2.kat | turtledraw 0.0 30.0 out.svg

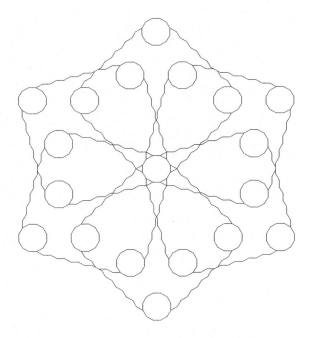

chseq 355 113 2808 | katrans t12.kat | turtledraw 0.0 60.0 out.svg

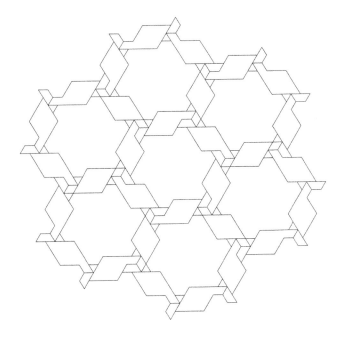

chseq 355 113 4212 | katrans t2.kat | turtledraw 0.0 80.0 out.svg

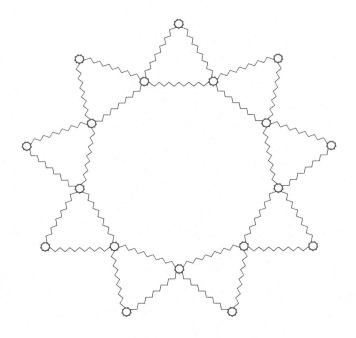

chseq 355 113 2808 | katrans t2.kat | turtledraw 0.0 45.0 out.svg

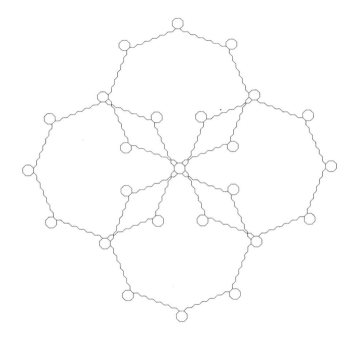

148

chseq 355 113 2808 | katrans t11.kat | turtledraw 0.0 45.0 out.svg

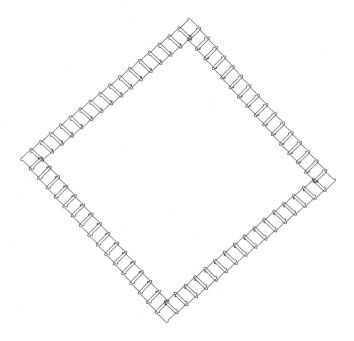

chseq 355 113 2808 | katrans t3.kat | turtledraw 0.0 170.0 out.svg

chseq 355 113 3744 | katrans t13.kat | turtledraw 0.0 90.0 out.svg

chseq 103993 33102 3917 | katrans t10.kat | turtledraw 0.0 45.0 out.svg

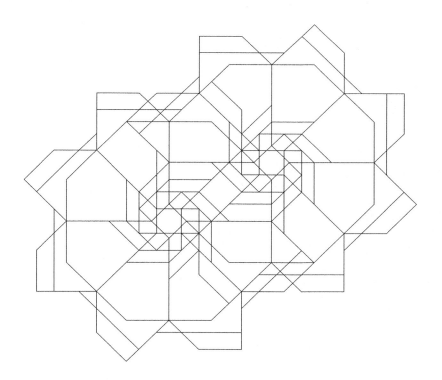

`chseq 103993 33102 3917 | katrans t0b.kat | turtledraw 0.0 60.0 out.svg`

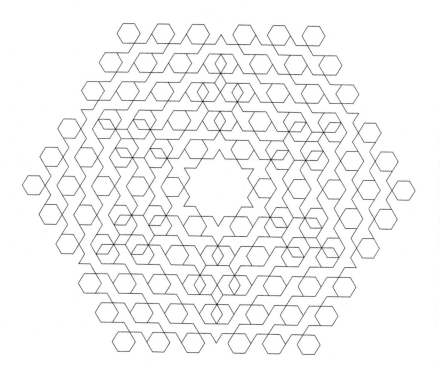

chseq 103993 33102 3917 | katrans t1.kat | turtledraw 0.0 60.0 out.svg

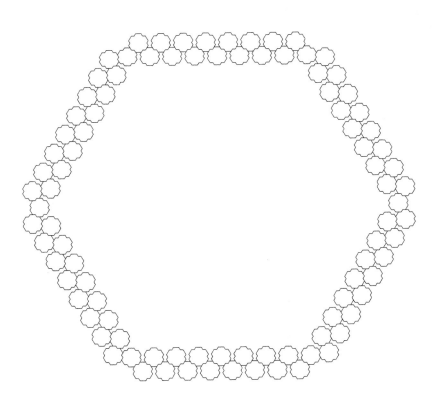

154

chseq 103993 33102 3917 | katrans t1.kat | turtledraw 0.0 90.0 out.svg

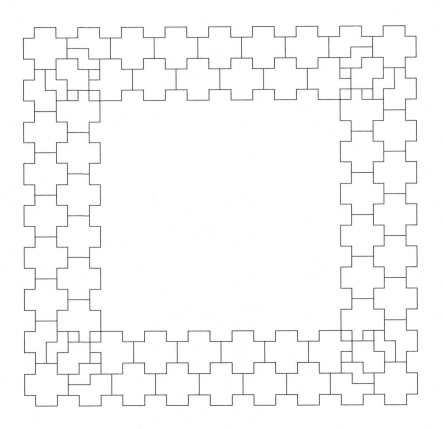

chseq 103993 33102 3917 | katrans t2.kat | turtledraw 0.0 90.0 out.svg

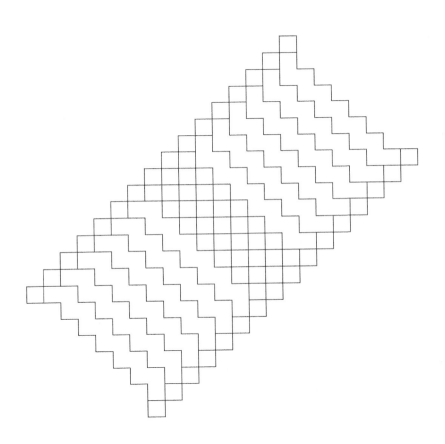

chseq 103993 33102 3917 | katrans t12.kat | turtledraw 0.0 90.0 out.svg

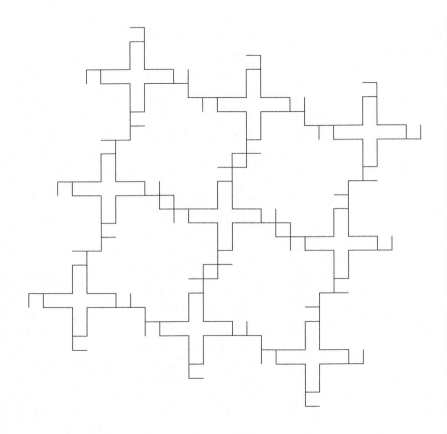

Another transcendental number is e, the base of the natural logarithm. Its value to 20 decimal places is $e = 2.71828182845904523536\ldots$ Its continued fraction is $e = [2,1,2,1,1,4,1,1,6,1,1,8,1,1,10,\ldots]$. The pattern of two 1's followed by $4,6,8,10,12,\ldots$ continues forever. The first few convergents of e are shown in the table below followed by some images that can be generated from them.

e	$2.71828182845904523536\ldots$
$\frac{8}{3}$	2.66666666666666666666
$\frac{11}{4}$	2.75000000000000000000
$\frac{19}{7}$	2.71428571428571428571
$\frac{87}{32}$	2.71875000000000000000
$\frac{106}{39}$	2.71794871794871794871
$\frac{193}{71}$	2.71830985915492957746
$\frac{1264}{465}$	2.71827956989247311827
$\frac{1457}{536}$	2.71828358208955223880
$\frac{2721}{1001}$	2.71828171828171828171
$\frac{23225}{8544}$	2.71828183520599250936

chseq 1264 465 10374 | katrans t1.kat | turtledraw 0.0 45.0 out.svg

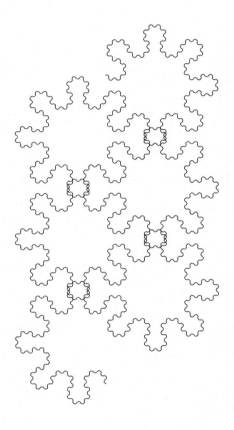

chseq 11 4 120 | katrans t6.kat | turtledraw 0.0 45.0 out.svg

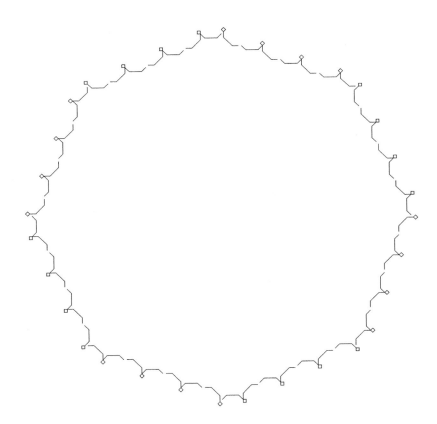

chseq 1264 465 1729 | katrans t2.kat | turtledraw 0.0 60.0 out.svg

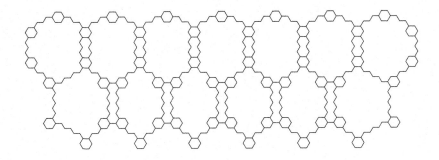

chseq 1264 465 1729 | katrans t12.kat | turtledraw 0.0 60.0 out.svg

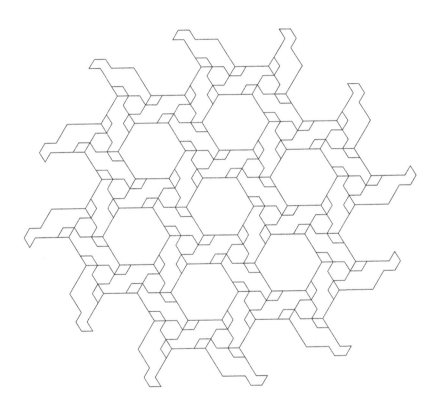

chseq 11 4 150 | katrans t0.kat | turtledraw 0.0 170.0 out.svg

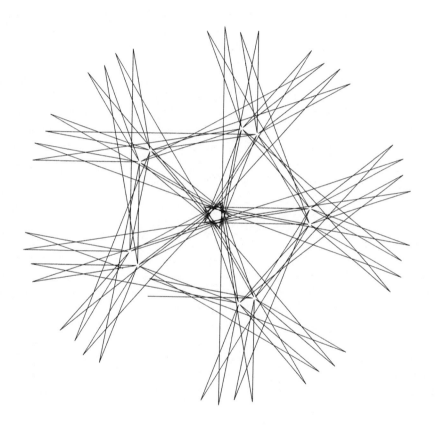

chseq 19 7 468 | katrans t8.kat | turtledraw 0.0 170.0 out.svg

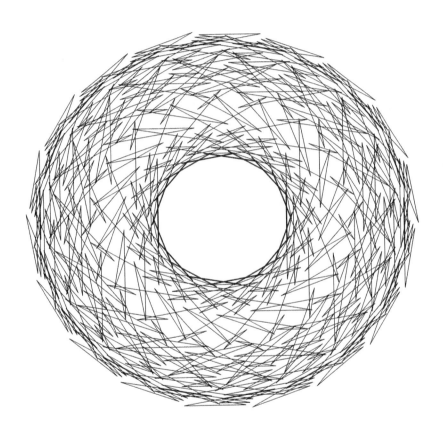

164

chseq 87 32 476 | katrans t15.kat | turtledraw 0.0 170.0 out.svg

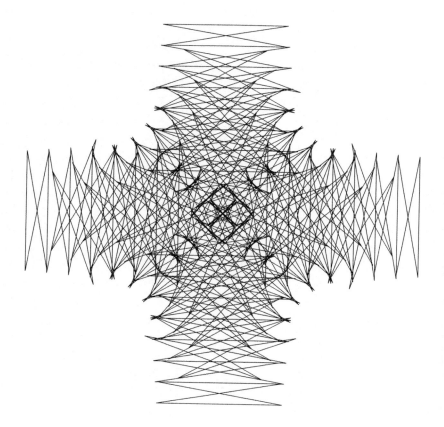

The Euler-Mascheroni constant appears in probability, statistics, physics, number theory, and mathematical analysis. Whether it's an irrational or transcendental number is still not known. Its value to 20 decimal places is

$\gamma = 0.57721566490153286061\ldots$.

Its continued fraction is

$\gamma = [0, 1, 1, 2, 1, 2, 1, 4, 3, 13, 5, 1, 1, 8, \ldots]$.

Like π there is no discernible pattern to the terms and since it is not known for sure if γ is irrational we don't know if the terms go on forever or stop at some point. The odds are good that it is irrational and the terms never stop. The first few convergents are shown in the table below, followed by some of the images you can generate from them.

γ	$0.57721566490153286061\ldots$
$\frac{4}{7}$	0.57142857142857142857
$\frac{11}{19}$	0.57894736842105263157
$\frac{15}{26}$	0.57692307692307692307
$\frac{71}{123}$	0.57723577235772357723
$\frac{228}{395}$	0.57721518987341772151
$\frac{3035}{5258}$	0.57721567135793077215
$\frac{15403}{26685}$	0.57721566423084129660
$\frac{18438}{31943}$	0.57721566540400087656
$\frac{33841}{58628}$	0.57721566487002797298

chseq 71 123 388 | katrans t0.kat | turtledraw 0.0 170.0 out.svg

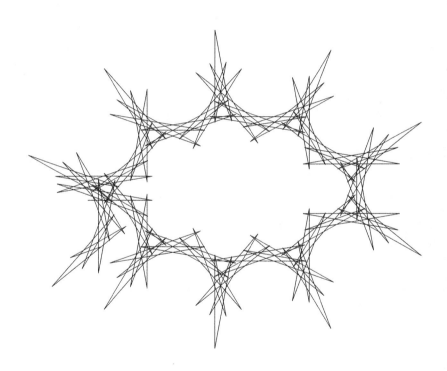

chseq 15 26 164 | katrans t0a.kat | turtledraw 0.0 45.0 out.svg

chseq 11 19 240 | katrans t5.kat | turtledraw 0.0 45.0 out.svg

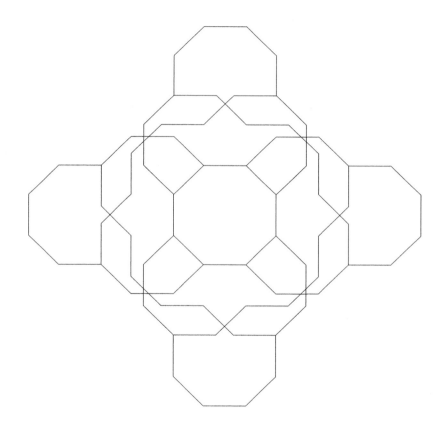

chseq 228 295 523 | katrans t8.kat | turtledraw 0.0 45.0 out.svg

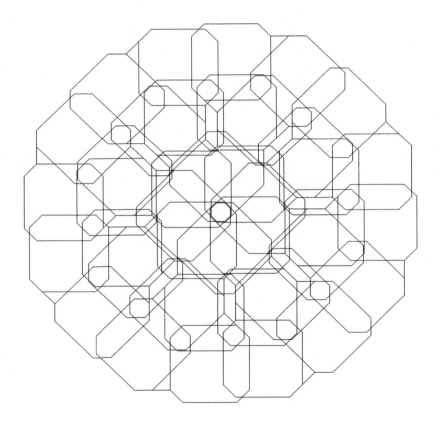

chseq 228 295 523 | katrans t2.kat | turtledraw 0.0 60.0 out.svg

chseq 15 26 328 | katrans t7.kat | turtledraw 0.0 60.0 out.svg

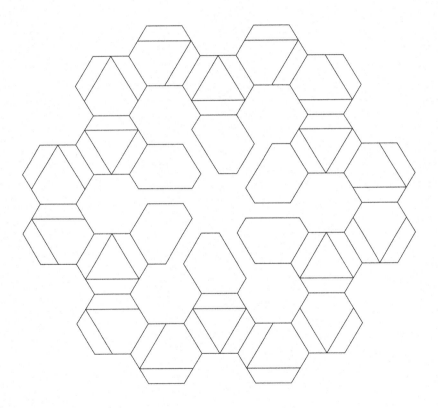

chseq 228 295 3138 | katrans t7.kat | turtledraw 0.0 60.0 out.svg

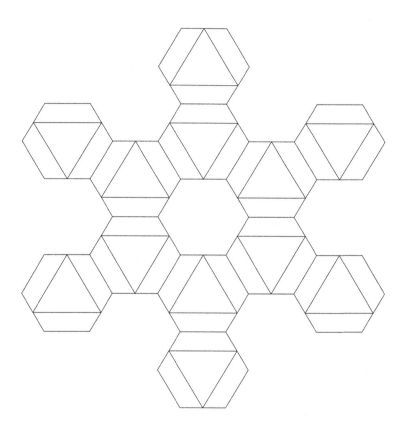

chseq 71 123 582 | katrans t8.kat | turtledraw 0.0 60.0 out.svg

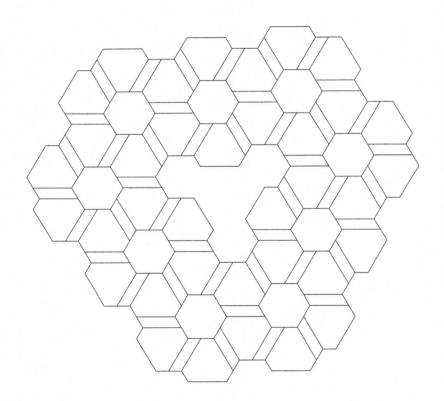

chseq 228 295 523 | katrans t15.kat | turtledraw 0.0 90.0 out.svg

AUTOMATIC SEQUENCES

Automatic sequences are another class of sequences that can be used to generate patterns. To find the nth term in an automatic sequence, you expand the number n in a base $b \geq 2$ number system and then feed the resulting digits into a finite automaton. Each state of the automaton must have b transitions to the other states corresponding to the different possible digits. Each state also has an output associated with it, just like the translation automata that we used to convert Christoffel words into drawing instructions. The difference is that output is only produced by the final state of the automaton. The final state is reached when the last digit is read. The best way to illustrate this is with an example.

The Thue-Morse sequence is probably the most well known and studied automatic sequence. It is named for *Axel Thue* (1863-1922) and *Marston Morse* (1892-1977). Axel Thue published a paper on the sequence in 1906 that is usually regarded as founding the mathematical subject of combinatorics on words. His work however was not widely known until 1921 when Marston Morse used the sequence in a paper on differential geometry.

There are many ways to define the Thue-Morse sequence. As an automatic sequence, the nth term is calculated by counting the number of 1's in the binary representation of n. If the number of 1's is even, then the nth term is equal to 0, otherwise it's equal to 1. An automaton for producing the sequence is shown below.

Figure 12: Axel Thue (1863-1922). Photo credit: wikipedia.org

Figure 13: Marston Morse (1892-1977). Photo credit: Mathematisches Forschungsinstitut Oberwolfach GmbH

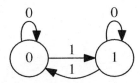

The automaton starts in state 0 and you feed it the binary representation of n. If it ends in state 0, it outputs a 0. If it ends in state 1, it outputs a 1. The table shows how the first 10 elements of the sequence are produced.

n	binary	1's count	output
0	0	0	0
1	1	1	1
2	10	1	1
3	11	2	0
4	100	1	1
5	101	2	0
6	110	2	0
7	111	3	1
8	1000	1	1
9	1001	2	0

The first 40 elements of the sequence are:
0110100110010110100101100110100110010110

The following snippet of C code calculates the first n terms of the sequence:

```
unsigned int i, j, k, n;

for(i=0; i<n; ++i)
  {
    for(j=i, k=0; j>0; j>>=1) if(j & 1) ++k;
    putchar(k & 1 ? '1' : '0');
  }
```

Another way to generate the sequence is to start with 0 and then repeatedly apply the following substitutions: $0 \to 01$, $1 \to 10$. This produces words in the following order: 0, 01, 0110, 01101001, and so on. This method is similar to the L-system method for generating fractal images that we will look at in a later chapter. The sequence also has a fractal structure. If you delete every odd numbered element in the sequence, you are once again left with the sequence.

You can also see the fractal structure in some of the images generated by the sequence. Just as with Christoffel words, you turn the sequence into a drawing by using an automaton translator to convert the 1's and 0's into drawing instructions. The simplest translator just turns a 0 into F and 1 into +F. The automaton file for doing this is t0.kat which is listed in appendix A. The following two images show the results of using the translation for sequences of length 255 and 1023.

The images appear to be a baroque form of the Koch curve which we will look at in the L-system chapter.

tmseq 255 | katrans t0.kat | turtledraw -60.0 60.0 out.svg

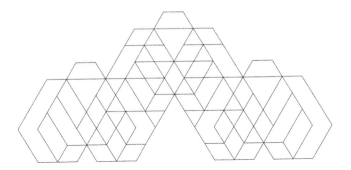

```
tmseq 1023 | katrans t0.kat | turtledraw -60.0 60.0 out.svg
```

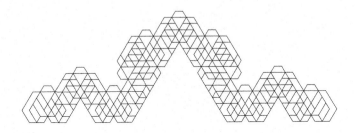

Using other forms of the simple t0.kat translator,
t0a,b,c.kat which are listed in appendix A, will give
you the following images.

tmseq 256 | katrans t0a.kat | turtledraw 120.0 60.0 out.svg

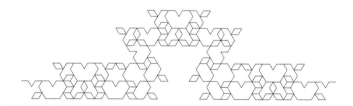

`tmseq 1024 | katrans t0a.kat | turtledraw 120.0 60.0 out.svg`

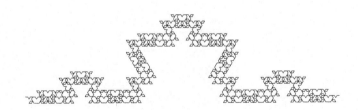

tmseq 256 | katrans t0b.kat | turtledraw 60.0 60.0 out.svg

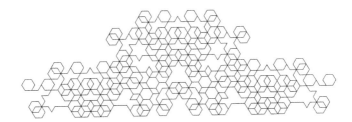

tmseq 1024 | katrans t0b.kat | turtledraw 60.0 60.0 out.svg

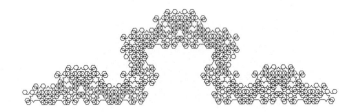

`tmseq 1024 | katrans t0c.kat | turtledraw 120.0 60.0 out.svg`

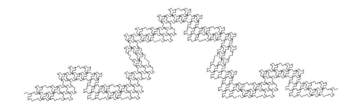

The following are examples of using other translators (listed in appendix A) on the sequence.

```
tmseq 257 | katrans t8.kat | turtledraw 65.0 170.0 out.svg
```

tmseq 512 | katrans t9.kat | turtledraw 10.0 170.0 out.svg

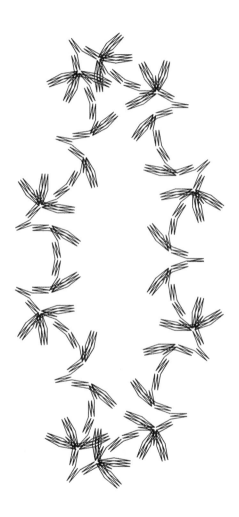

`tmseq 512 | katrans t9.kat | turtledraw -40.0 175.00 out.svg`

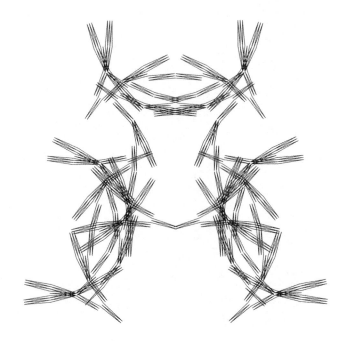

`tmseq 512 | katrans t9.kat | turtledraw 120.0 60.0 out.svg`

tmseq 514 | katrans t9.kat | turtledraw -80.0 35.00 out.svg

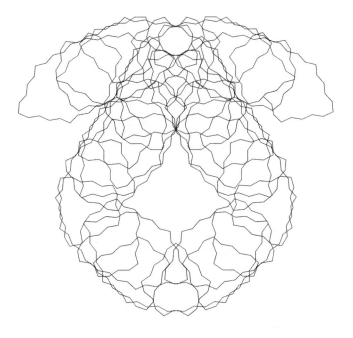

tmseq 289 | katrans t13.kat | turtledraw 0.0 30.0 out.svg

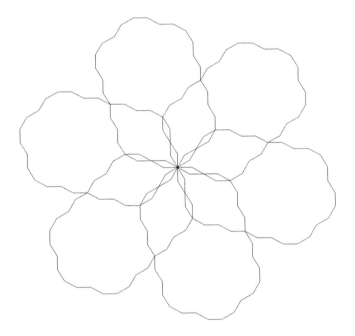

tmseq 1000 | katrans t13.kat | turtledraw 0.0 175.00 out.svg

`tmseq 2048 | katrans t14.kat | turtledraw 22.5 45.00 out.svg`

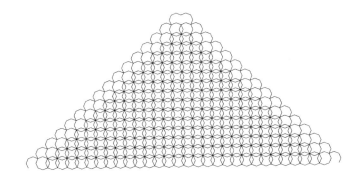

tmseq 128 | katrans t15.kat | turtledraw -30.0 60.0 out.svg

tmseq 720 | katrans t15.kat | turtledraw 0.0 170.0 out.svg

Another automatic sequence that can be used to generate patterns is called the Rudin-Shapiro sequence. It is named after American mathematicians *Walter Rudin* (1921-2010) and *Harold S. Shapiro* (1928-). The nth term in the sequence is generated by counting the number of occurrences of 11 in the binary expansion of n. The 11's can be overlapping so that 111 counts as two occurrences of 11. If the number of occurrences is even, then the nth term is equal to 1, otherwise it's 0. The sequence is often expressed in terms of $+1$'s and -1's whereas we have expressed it in terms of 1's and 0's. To convert from our form to the other form, use the formula $2b - 1$ where b is a term in the sequence as we have defined it. The following snippet of C code will calculate the first n terms of the sequence:

```
unsigned int i, j, k, n;

for(i=0; i<n; ++i)
  {
    for(j=i, k=0; j>0; j>>=1) if((j & 3) == 3) ++k;
    putchar(k & 1 ? '0' : '1');
  }
```

The following are some examples of patterns generated with the Rudin-Shapiro sequence.

rsseq 2732 | katrans t14.kat | turtledraw 45.0 90.0 out.svg

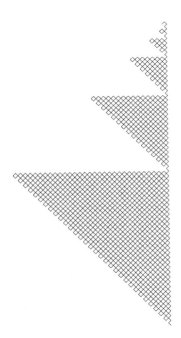

rsseq 683 | katrans t14.kat | turtledraw -30.0 60.0 out.svg

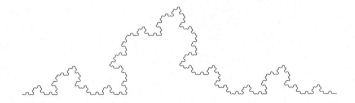

Instead of using algorithmically generated binary sequences as above, we can also use randomly generated sequences. The program rndseq can be used to generate such sequences. It takes one input, the number of digits to generate, and an optional input, a seed integer for the random number generator. If the seed integer is not supplied, then a different random binary string is produced every time. If one is supplied, then the same random binary string is produced. This can be useful to re-generate interesting drawings you find. Some examples are shown below.

rndseq 500 422321 | katrans t1.kat | turtledraw 0.0 45.0 out.svg

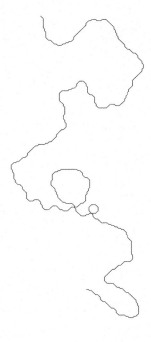

rndseq 500 59 | katrans t15.kat | turtledraw 0.0 45.0 out.svg

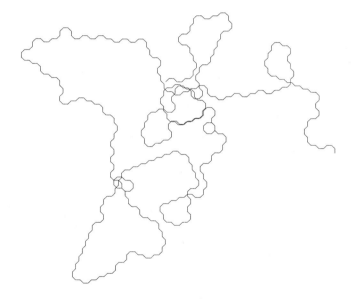

rndseq 500 24043 | katrans t15.kat | turtledraw 0.0 60.0 out.svg

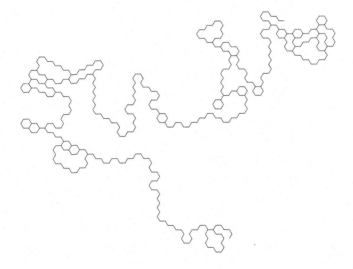

rndseq 500 1259 | katrans t1.kat | turtledraw 0.0 170.0 out.svg

rndseq 500 59 | katrans t6.kat | turtledraw 0.0 170.0 out.svg

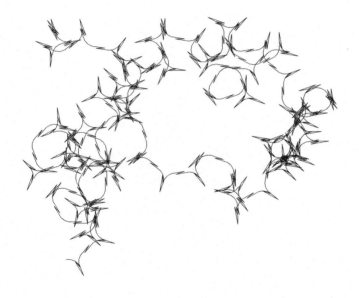

PAPER FOLDING

A large class of binary sequences can be generated using the idea of paper folding. Put a rectangular strip of paper on a flat surface in front of you with the long dimension going left to right. Now pick up the right end of the paper and fold it over onto the left end. Repeat this process a few times and then unfold the paper. What you will see is a sequence of creases in the paper, some will look like valleys and some will look like ridges. With one fold there will be a single valley in the middle after unfolding. With two folds you will have three creases of type: valley, valley, ridge, from left to right. Three folds gives you 7 creases and in general n folds gives you $2^n - 1$ creases. With a real sheet of paper it is hard to get more than five or six folds but mathematically you can fold as many times as you like and it is easy to predict the resulting sequence of creases.

Let valley creases be symbolized by the number 1 and ridge creases by the number 0 then the sequence of creases after 1, 2, 3, and 4 folds will look like:
1
110
1101100
110110011100100
Looking at this series of sequences you may notice that the next sequence is found by adding a 1 to the end of

the current sequence and then reflecting it about the
end point with 1's and 0's interchanged. Take for example the second sequence, 110, and add a 1 to the
end to get 1101. Now reverse 110 with 1's and 0's interchanged to get 100. Add this to 1101 to get the next
sequence 1101100. For any sequence in the series, this
procedure gives you the next sequence. To formalize
the process let S_n be the sequence of creases after n
folds and let $\overline{S_n^R}$ represent the reverse of the sequence
with 1's and 0's interchanged, then the next sequence
is $S_{n+1} = S_n\, 1\, \overline{S_n^R}$.

The next sequence always has the previous sequence as
a prefix, we are just adding new terms onto the end.
This means that if you continue folding forever you will
produce a unique infinite sequence of creases. In other
words, there is a unique S_∞ which is called the regular
paper folding sequence. The sequence out to 31 terms
is

$$S_\infty = 1101100111001001110110000110010\ldots$$

It is possible to calculate the individual terms in S_∞
directly. Let c_n be the nth term in the sequence then
its value can be calculated directly from the value of
n. Any integer n can be expressed in the form

$$n = 2^k(2j + 1)$$

The term $2j + 1$ is the odd part of n, meaning it is an
odd number. When an odd number is divided by 4 it

will have a remainder of 1 or 3 which we symbolize as $(2j + 1) \equiv 1 \mod 4$ and $(2j + 1) \equiv 3 \mod 4$. The value of c_n is then given by

$$c_n = \begin{cases} 1 & \text{if } (2j + 1) \equiv 1 \mod 4 \\ 0 & \text{if } (2j + 1) \equiv 3 \mod 4 \end{cases}$$

The program `pfold` will generate the regular paper folding sequence. It takes 3 parameters and is called like this:

```
pfold n m f
```

The first parameter, `n`, is the number of terms you want to calculate. To get the complete sequence for k folds you should set `n=` $2^k - 1$. The other 2 parameters can be used to generate a variety of different paper folding sequences which we will discuss below. For the regular paper folding sequence set `m=` 1 and `f=` 1.

Once you have generated the sequence you can convert it to drawing instructions like we did with the other sequences discussed so far. You can set the drawing instructions so that the drawing will resemble the actual shape of the unfolded paper by converting a 1 to $-F$ and a 0 to $+F$. The translation automaton file for this is called `pf0.kat` and is listed in appendix A. If you use a turn angle of 90 degrees then the drawing will look like the shape of the paper when each fold is unfolded to 90 degrees and you are looking at the paper edge on.

Calculating the first 4095 terms of the sequence and translating using `pf0.kat` produces the famous *dragon curve* fractal shown in the figure below. This corresponds to folding the paper 12 times which you probably can't do with an actual piece of paper. Note that if you reduce the drawing turn angle to say 70 degrees then you are essentially flattening out the paper more from its folded state and you will get something that looks like the next figure which is also a fractal curve.

pfold 4095 1 3 | katrans pf0.kat | turtledraw 90.0 90.0 out.svg

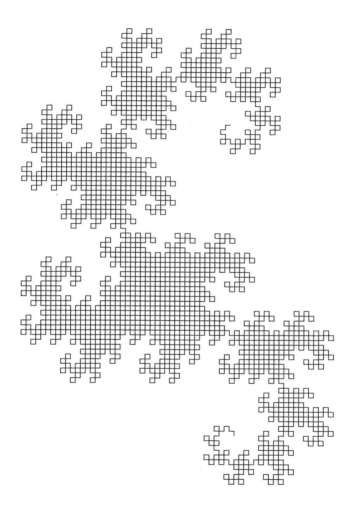

pfold 4095 1 3 | katrans pf0.kat | turtledraw 0.0 70.0 out.svg

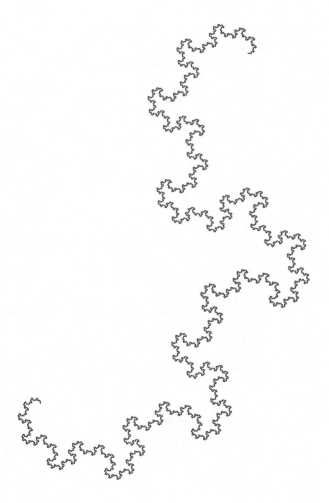

The regular paper folding sequence results from folding the paper in the same direction all the time. If you fold the paper in alternating directions, or you use some other series of folds, then you will get a different sequence. If the paper is folded in alternating directions then you will get the following series of sequences after 1, 2, 3, and 4 folds:

1

100

1001110

100111001000110

Like the regular paper folding sequence, you can get the next sequence in the series by adding a term to the end and reflecting the sequence about that term with 1's and 0's interchanged. The difference is that the terms added to the end alternate between 1 and 0. So for example $S_3 = S_2 1 \overline{S_2^R}$ while $S_4 = S_3 0 \overline{S_3^R}$. In the limit as you do the alternate folding an infinite number of times, you once again get a unique sequence S_∞ called the alternating paper folding sequence.

Instead of using alternating folds, you can use any pattern of folds. Let a_k indicate the direction of the kth fold. It can have two values: 1 or 0. In the regular paper folding sequence, all the a_k are equal to 1. In the alternating paper folding sequence, they alternate between 1 and 0. Given the a_k values, you can calculate the terms in the resulting paper folding sequence using the following formula

$$c_n = \begin{cases} a_k & \text{if } (2j+1) \equiv 1 \mod 4 \\ 1 - a_k & \text{if } (2j+1) \equiv 3 \mod 4 \end{cases}$$

where the k and j values come from factoring n into the form $n = 2^k(2j+1)$.

So all we need to generate general paper folding sequences is a series of folding instructions, the a_k values. The simplest thing to do is to use a periodic sequence of binary values for a_k. These can come from the binary expansion of a given number f which we will call the folding function. To fully specify the folding function, you need not just the value of f but also a size value indicating how many bits are used to represent f. Call the size value m then f will be represented with m bits and can have a value from 0 to $2^m - 1$.

For example if $m = 1$ then f is represented by 1 bit and can have only two values: 0 and 1. The binary representation of these values is also 0 and 1. For the regular paper folding sequence we used $m = 1$ and $f = 1$ so that in binary $f = 1$ and all the a_k values equal 1. The alternating paper folding sequence can be generated with $m = 2$ and $f = 1$ so that in binary $f = 01$ and the a_k values, starting with $k = 0$, are 10101010.... The value of m is important since it can change how f is represented and thereby change the values of a_k. For example if $m = 4$ and $f = 3$ then f is represented in binary as $f = 0011$, and the a_k values, starting with $k = 0$, are $110011001100\ldots$.

Note that the a_k values, starting with $k = 0$, are found by writing the binary representation of f backwards and repeating it. This means that a_k will equal bit $i = k \bmod m$ of f. The program `pfold` will do all these calculations for you and generate the resulting paper folding sequence. You call it like this:

`pfold n m f`

where `n` is the number of terms to generate, `m` is the size of the binary representation of the folding function and `f` is the folding function number which can range from 0 to $2^m - 1$.

Now let's look at some more examples. For the alternating paper folding sequence, use $n = 2047$, $m = 2$, $f = 1$, the `pf0.kat` translator and a drawing angle of $90°$. The result is the picture on the following page. Changing the drawing angle to $85°$ produces the next picture. In terms of an unfolded piece of paper, the second picture is slightly more unfolded than the first.

After the alternating paper folding sequence are more examples using various values of f with $m = 32$, $n = 2047$, the `pf0.kat` translator and a drawing angle of $90°$.

pfold 2047 2 1 | katrans pf0.kat | turtledraw 0.0 90.0 out.svg

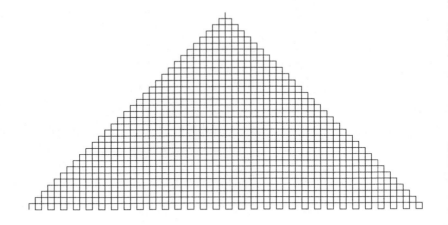

pfold 2047 2 1 | katrans pf0.kat | turtledraw 0.0 85.0 out.svg

pfold 2047 32 3016850367 | katrans pf0.kat |
turtledraw 0.0 90.0 out.svg

pfold 2047 32 2421739082 | katrans pf0.kat |
turtledraw 0.0 90.0 out.svg

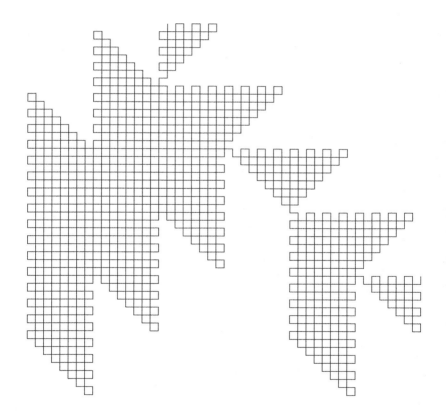

```
pfold 2047 32 4000080373 | katrans pf0.kat |
turtledraw 0.0 90.0 out.svg
```

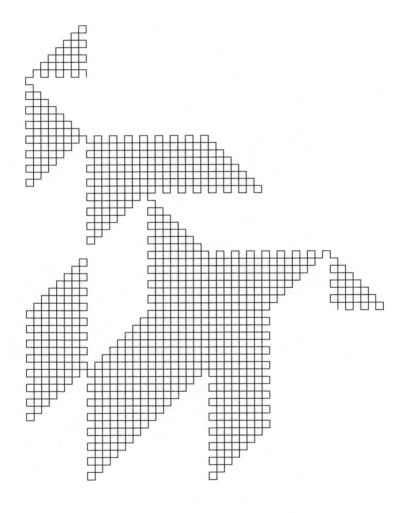

pfold 2047 32 3351491713 | katrans pf0.kat |
turtledraw 0.0 90.0 out.svg

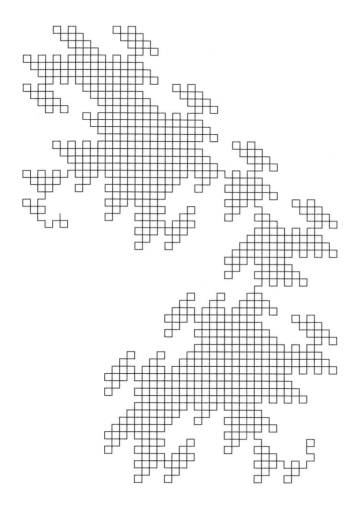

```
pfold 2047 32 3562271007 | katrans pf0.kat |
  turtledraw 0.0 90.0 out.svg
```

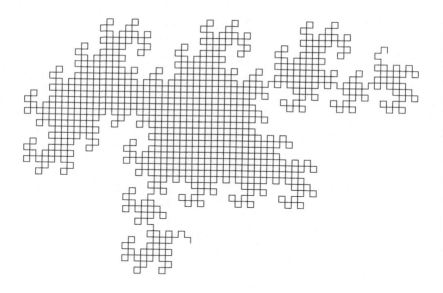

pfold 2047 32 3506884879 | katrans pf0.kat |
turtledraw 0.0 90.0 out.svg

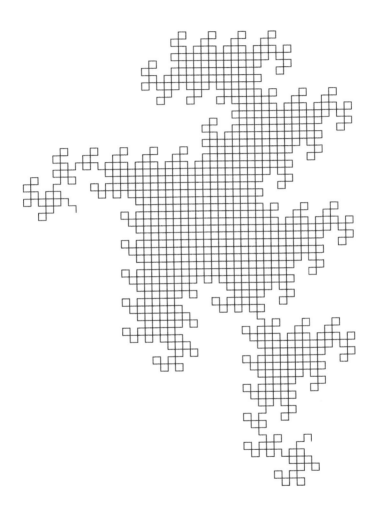

pfold 2047 32 2448489033 | katrans pf0.kat |
turtledraw 0.0 90.0 out.svg

pfold 2047 32 3685592511 | katrans pf0.kat |
 turtledraw 0.0 90.0 out.svg

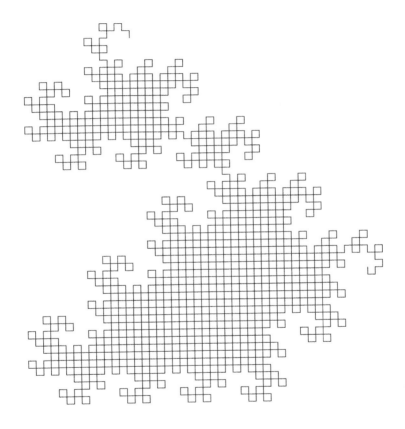

pfold 2047 32 3643706774 | katrans pf0.kat |
turtledraw 0.0 90.0 out.svg

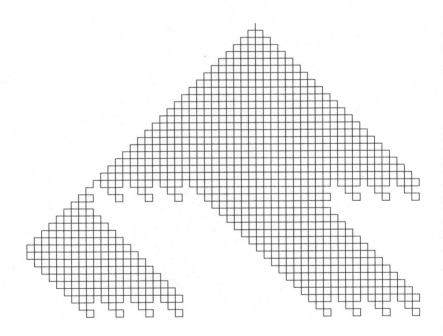

```
pfold 2047 32 3648678492 | katrans pf0.kat |
 turtledraw 0.0 90.0 out.svg
```

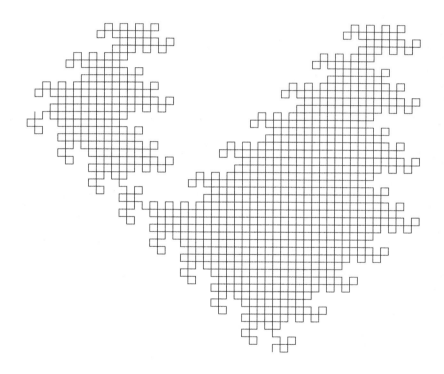

pfold 2047 32 2294411176 | katrans pf0.kat |
turtledraw 0.0 90.0 out.svg

Lindenmayer Systems

FORMAL DEFINITION

An L-system is a type of formal language. Formal languages have long been used in the theory of algorithms and computation and there is an extensive body of literature on them. A formal language consists of a set of symbols, called an alphabet, together with a set of rules, call a grammar. The grammar can be used to generate the words of the language or it can be used to determine if a word is in the language. Words are just strings of symbols from the alphabet.

Let V denote the alphabet of an L-system, then we define it as follows:

$$V = \{a_1, a_2, a_3, \ldots, a_n\}$$

The a_i's are the symbols that compose the alphabet. In general any set of symbols can be used to make up the alphabet. For instance, many of the L-systems in this book have alphabets containing the symbols $F, f, +, -, [,]$. We will use the a_i symbols for now to keep things as general as possible.

Let's call a string of symbols from the alphabet a word and denote the set of all possible words that can be constructed from V by the letter W. The following shows some of the words contained in W:

$$W = \{a_1, a_1 a_2, a_1 a_3, a_2 a_3, a_1 a_2 a_3, \ldots\}$$

Even though V may be finite, W will contain an infinite number of elements.

An L-system begins with a word from the set W called the axiom. A set of rules for replacing the symbols in the axiom by other symbols or groups of symbols is then used to generate another word in W. The same process is then applied to this new word to generate the next word and so on. L-systems are also sometimes called rewriting systems because of this process of rewriting words, using a set of rules, to form new words. The rules in L-system theory are usually called productions and we will use this term for the remainder of the book. The general form of a production is as follows:

$$a_i \rightarrow P(a_i)$$

where $P(a_i)$ is an element of the set W. This rule, in words, says that all occurrences of the symbol a_i should be replaced by the word $P(a_i)$ from W. All the symbols in the alphabet do not need to have an explicit production rule associated with them. If a symbol does not have a production rule it is assumed that the symbol is copied into the new word as is, without being replaced by anything else. This is equivalent to assuming the following production rule exists for the symbol:

$$a_i \rightarrow a_i$$

Now let's look at an example of a simple L-system. The

alphabet will contain only two symbols.

$$V = \{a, b\}$$

For an axiom we will use the single symbol a. For production rules we will use the following:

$a \rightarrow ab$

$b \rightarrow ba$

Applying these production rules to our axiom, a, the following series of strings is generated.

Axiom : a

ab

$abba$

$abbabaab$

$abbabaabbaababba$

$\cdots$

It is important to remember that we can choose any word, composed of symbols from the alphabet, as our axiom. A different axiom will however, generate a different sequence of words. If we had chosen b as the axiom the following sequence of words would have been generated:

Axiom : *b*

       ba

       baab

       baababba

       baababbaabbabaab

       . . .

which obviously differs from the above sequence. If you compare the two sequences you'll see that you can go from one to the other by swapping *a* and *b* symbols. This is true because the productions remain the same when you swap *a*'s and *b*'s and the process was started by swapping the *a* in the axiom for a *b*. Also note that these sequences can are really just the Thue-Morse sequence in disguise. You get the Thue-Morse sequence by identifying the *a*'s and *b*'s with 1's and 0's.

Axioms are also not limited to single symbol words. If *baab* is chosen as the axiom then the sequence of words generated will proceed as above but starting with *baab* and not *b*. Choosing *aa* as the axiom will generate a sequence altogether different from the above two.

Axiom :   *aa*

 abab

 abbaabba

 abbabaababbabaab

 abbabaabbaababbaabbabaabbaababba

 . . .

Note that each word in this sequence is composed of two copies of words in the first sequence above. This is because we used an axiom that is two copies of the first axiom. The point is that the same production rules can generate different sequences of words by starting with different axioms.

As a final example let's look at the case where some of the symbols in the alphabet do not have explicit production rules. For this example we will use the following alphabet, axiom, and production rule:

$$V = \{a, b, c\}$$

Axiom :   *aca*

$$a \to cab$$

Applying the production rule to the axiom generates

the following sequence of words:

Axiom : *aca*

cabccab

ccabbcccabb

ccccabbbbcccccabbbb

. . .

The implicit production rules in this sequence are:

$b \rightarrow b$

$c \rightarrow c$

GRAPHICAL INTERPRETATION

An L-system, by itself, is just a method for generating a string of symbols according to a set of rules. In order to make the string of symbols represent a graphical object, such as a plant drawing, we must give a graphical interpretation to each of the symbols in the string. The metaphor we will use to interpret the symbols is that of drawing on a paper with a mechanical pen controlled by commands. Each symbol in the L-system alphabet will represent a command used to control the pen. The string generated by the L-system will then cause the pen to execute a series of commands that will result in a figure being drawn.

One of the most basic commands we can give a pen is to move forward in a straight line a certain distance. The term, moving forward, is used in the sense that we assume the pen has a direction associated with it and when it receives a command to move forward it moves in that direction. At the very least we must also be able to change the direction in which the pen will move. A change in direction can be either clockwise or counterclockwise from the current direction.

Let us now assign symbols to represent these basic commands. The move forward command will be assigned the symbol F. When the pen is fed the symbol F it will move forward a fixed distance, drawing a straight line on the page. We will call the fixed distance the pen moves, the stroke length. Clockwise and counterclockwise changes in direction will be assigned the symbols − and + respectively. When the pen is fed the symbol − it will change direction by a fixed angular amount in the clockwise direction. When the pen is fed the symbol + it will change direction by a fixed angular amount in the counterclockwise direction. We will call the fixed angular change in direction the turn angle. For a stroke length d and turn angle θ the symbol definitions can be summarized as follows:

F = move forward a distance d

− = change direction clockwise by angle θ

+ = change direction counterclockwise by angle θ

Using just these three symbols we can already command the pen to draw a variety of shapes. If we use a turn angle of 90 degrees then the string $F + F + F + F$ will cause the pen to draw a square. Assuming the direction of the pen is initially horizontal toward the right edge of the paper, the string will draw the square in the following manner:

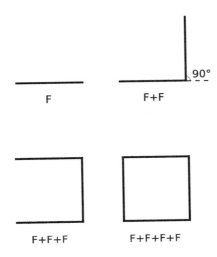

For the string $F + F - F - F + F$ the pen will execute
the following movements:

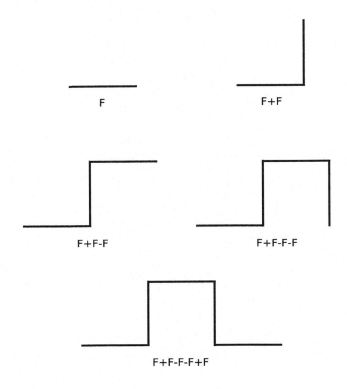

By changing the turn angle, the same string will draw different shapes. Using a turn angle of 120 degrees for example, will cause the pen to draw a triangle when presented with the string $F + F + F$.

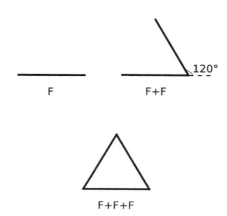

In general we can draw an n sided polygon by setting the turn angle to $360/n$ degrees and then feeding the pen a string of n move forward commands (F) separated by change direction commands ($+$). The following table illustrates this for several polygons.

n	Turn angle	String	Polygon
3	120	F+F+F	Triangle
4	90	F+F+F+F	Square
5	72	F+F+F+F+F	Pentagon
6	60	F+F+F+F+F+F	Hexagon

Table 1: Turn angle and string for 3 to 6 sided polygons.

So far we have considered only single strings of symbols (pen commands). We will now look at how an L-system can be used to generate a desired string. Let us begin by reviewing the basic ideas behind an L-system. An L-system begins with a string of symbols from its alphabet called the axiom. It then uses a set of substitutions called production rules to replace symbols in the string by other strings of symbols from the alphabet thus generating a new string. The process is then repeated on the new string to generate yet another string. Using this process a long complex string can be generated from a simple axiom and a few production rules.

As an example we will use an L-system to generate the string needed to draw a square as shown above. This L-system requires only one production rule and is defined below.

Turn Angle $= 90$

Axiom $= F + F$

Productions:

$F \rightarrow F + F$

Starting with the axiom and iterating the L-system once generates the following sequence:

Axiom: $\qquad F + F$

1st iteration: $\quad F + F + F + F$

Further iterations will just cause the pen to retrace the square. For another example, consider the following L-system which generates a hexagon.

Turn Angle $= 60$

Axiom $= F + F + F$

Productions:

$F \rightarrow F + F$

Starting with the axiom and iterating the L-system once generates the following sequence:

Axiom: $F + F + F$

1st iteration: $F + F + F + F + F + F$

Once again, further iterations will just cause the pen to retrace the hexagon.

Now that we have seen how L-systems can be used to draw simple polygons it is time to move on to more complex objects where the real power of L-systems becomes evident. We will begin by looking at how L-systems can be used to generate a class of objects called Koch curves.

KOCH CURVES

Koch curves are named after the Swedish mathematician Helge von Koch who first described them in a paper published in 1904 (*Sur une courbe continue sans tangente, obtenue par une construction géometrique élémentaire*, Arkiv för Matematik **1** (1904) 681-704). Koch curves have several interesting properties but we will be concerned with only one, the property of self-similarity or dilational symmetry.

An object that possesses the property of self similarity is composed of scaled down copies of itself. In other words, if we take a particular piece of the object and magnify it, it will look like the whole object. The original Koch curve shown below illustrates this concept.

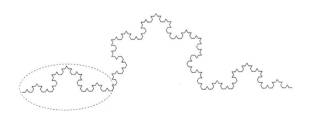

The self similarity of this Koch curve can be seen by comparing the circled region to the entire curve. The circled region appears to be a scaled down copy of the entire curve. It is not an exact copy because the curve shown in the figure is really only a finite approximation to the true Koch curve. The true Koch curve results when the steps in the construction process for the curve are iterated an infinite number of times. The first four steps in the construction of the Koch curve are shown below.

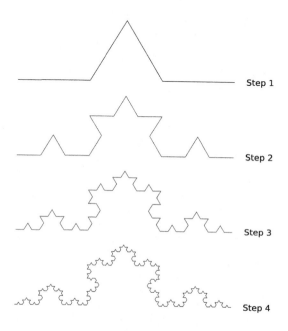

Step 1

Step 2

Step 3

Step 4

Notice that in going from step 1 to step 2, each straight line segment was replaced by a copy of the step 1 curve scaled by a factor of 1/3. The scaling is such that if straight line segments in step 1 have length = 1, then straight line segments in step 2 will have length = 1/3. The same procedure is used to go from step 2 to step 3.

Each straight line segment is replace by a copy of the step 1 curve scaled by a factor of 1/9. In general the procedure to go from step n to step $n+1$ is to replace all straight line segments in step n by copies of the step 1 curve scaled by a factor of $(1/3)^n$.

From the discussion in the last section we can see that this construction process for the Koch curve can be easily modeled using L-systems. The construction process merely replaces each straight line segment in a given step with a copy of the step 1 curve. This can be accomplished with L-systems by using a production for the move forward command, F, that will replace it with the command string needed to draw the step 1 curve. Using a turn angle of 60°, the string needed to generate the step 1 curve is $F + F - - F + F$. The geometric interpretation of this string is shown below.

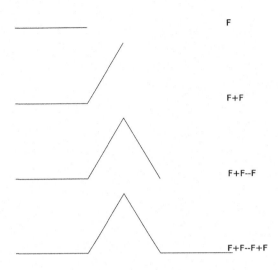

Using the production $F \to F + F - -F + F$ on this
string will generate the string needed to draw the second step:

$$\underline{F + F - -F + F} + \underline{F + F - -F + F} - -$$
$$\underline{F + F - -F + F} + \underline{F + F - -F + F}$$

The first step strings have been underlined. The geometric interpretation of this string is shown below.

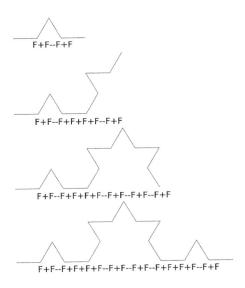

F+F--F+F

F+F--F+F+F+F--F+F

F+F--F+F+F+F--F+F--F+F--F+F

F+F--F+F+F+F--F+F--F+F--F+F+F+F+F--F+F

Once again applying the production to this string will generate the string for step 3 and so on. The complete definition for this L-system is as follows:

Koch curve

Turn Angle $= 60$

Axiom $= F$

Productions:

$$F \rightarrow F + F - - F + F$$

This L-system will start with a straight line, the axiom, and then generate step 1, step 2, step 3, and so on with each iteration. If we change the axiom to $F++F++F$, which is a triangle in this L-system, and switch the signs on the production rule to become $F \rightarrow F - F + +F - F$, then we will generate what is known as the Koch snowflake. The generation is shown below.

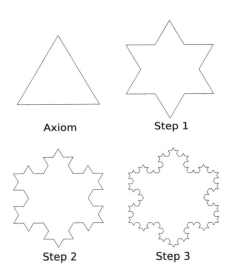

Axiom   Step 1

Step 2   Step 3

There are an almost limitless number of Koch-type curves that can be generated using L-systems. Examples of several Koch curves appear on the following pages.

The following Koch curve is called the three-segment curve because each straight line segment is replaced, in the next step, by a curve composed of three straight line segments scaled by a factor of $1/\sqrt{5}$. The L-system we will use to generate this curve starts with an axiom that generates a square. The complete definition of the L-system and its first few iterations are shown below.

Three segment Koch curve

Scale Factor $= 1/\sqrt{5}$

Turn Angle $= 30$

Axiom $= F + + + F + + + F + + + F$

Productions:

$F \to +F - - - F + + + F-$

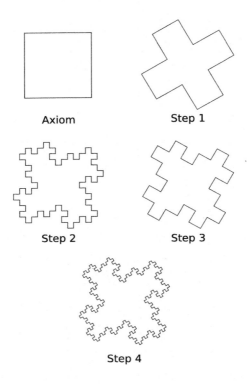

The next two curves are known as the eight and eighteen segment Koch curves respectively. Both L-systems use turn angles of 90° and axioms that generate squares.

Eight segment Koch curve

Scale Factor $= 1/4$

Turn Angle $= 90$

Axiom $= F + F + F + F$

Productions:

$F \rightarrow F + F - F - FF + F + F - F$

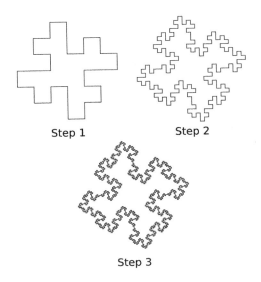

Step 1

Step 2

Step 3

Eighteen segment Koch curve

Scale Factor $= 1/6$

Turn Angle $= 90$

Axiom $= F + F + F + F$

Productions:

$F \rightarrow F + FF - FF - F - F + F + FF - F - F + F$
$+ FF + FF - F$

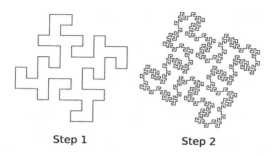

Step 1   Step 2

So far all the curves we have drawn are connected, i.e. they are drawn as one continuous line. To draw an unconnected curve we need to be able to move the pen without drawing a line. We will use the symbol f to represent the command to move forward a fixed distance without drawing a straight line. The symbol f is therefore identical to symbol F except that it does not cause a line to be drawn when the pen moves. Using this new symbol we can draw unconnected curves such as the one shown below.

Scale Factor $= 0.17$

Turn Angle $= 90$

Axiom $= F + F + F + F$

Productions:

$F \rightarrow F + f - FF + F + FF + Ff + FF - f + FF$
$\quad - F - FF - Ff - FFF$

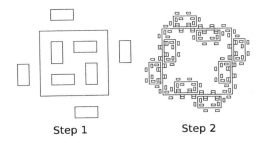

Step 1   Step 2

EDGE REWRITING

Let us refer to the lines drawn by the F symbol as edges. The productions for F act to replace, or rewrite, an edge when going from one step to the next. Having only one symbol to represent an edge is restrictive since it limits us to using the same production for all the edges. All the edges are therefore rewritten in the same way.

By introducing multiple edge symbols we can distinguish the edges from one another and use separate productions for each distinct edge. We will use the symbol G to also represent an edge, as F already does.

An example of an L-system with two distinct edges has productions:

$$F \rightarrow +G - F - G+$$
$$G \rightarrow -F + G + F-$$

Using a turn angle of 60° the following figure illustrates the productions.

259

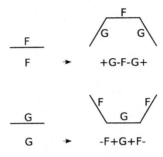

Using these productions the following L-system generates a curve known as the Sierpinski gasket.

Scale Factor $= 0.5$

Turn Angle $= 60$

Axiom $= F$

Productions:

$F \rightarrow +G - F - G+$

$G \rightarrow -F + G + F-$

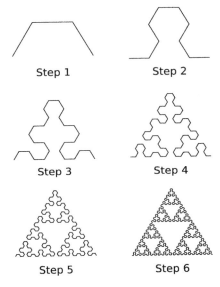

Step 1

Step 2

Step 3

Step 4

Step 5

Step 6

GENERATING IMAGES

Generating the images you have seen so far can be done with two programs we have written in the C programming language (there is a C language compiler for every major operating system). The first program `lsysgen` takes an L-system and generates a string of symbols that the second program `turtledraw` interprets as a drawing and produces an SVG (scalable vector graphics) file. Splitting this process into two parts as we have done may seem unnecessary, but it allows us more flexibility. For example, the string produced by an L-system may be interpreted not as a drawing, but as music. Or we might have a string from which the L-system that produced it is unknown (like the digits of π), but we nevertheless want to produce a drawing.

The first program `lsysgen` is run like this:

```
lsysgen file.ldf n
```

where `file.ldf` is an L-system definition file containing the axiom and production rule(s), and `n` is the number of times to iterate. For example, to iterate the Sierpinski gasket L-system six times, we feed `lsysgen` the file `sp.ldf` which contains the following four lines:

```
; Sierpinski gasket
F
F->+G-F-G+
```

```
G->-F+G+F-
```

and run the command like this:

```
lsysgen sp.ldf 6
```

When this command is run, you should see a long string consisting of the four symbols: $F, G, +, -$ that are output to the terminal. By default `lsysgen` sends its output to *standard output* (usually the terminal). Note that any number of comment lines are allowed at the start of the `ldf` file, specified by a semicolon in the first column.

Now that we have the output of `lsysgen`, we can feed it to `turtledraw` to produce an SVG image. This program gets its name from the computer graphics term *turtle graphics*. `turtledraw` is run like this:

```
turtledraw angle dangle file.svg
```

where `angle` is the start angle, `dangle` the increment or turn angle, and `file.svg` the output SVG file. The input to this program is *standard input* (stdin), which means that we can directly feed the output of `lsysgen` to the input of `turtledraw`. For example, to draw the Sierpinski gasket L-system string created above, we run the following:

```
lsysgen sp.ldf 6 | turtledraw 0.0 60.0 sp.svg
```

giving us the SVG file `sp.svg` which can be viewed

in a web browser like Firefox, or a graphics program like `display` from *Imagemagick*, or a vector graphics editing program like Inkscape. The resulting image is shown below.

INTRODUCING AUTOGEN

In this chapter we introduce a tool which we will use for a systematic exploration of the wonderland of L-system graphics. This tool is a program called autogen. Its power extends far beyond L-system graphics, but that is what we will use it for here. The program generates all words of a given length that are accepted by an automaton. This may sound rather dry, but it allows us to generate every possible L-system production rule of a specified form. All we must do is specify the form of the production rule we're interested in, and the program generates every possibility. The form of the production rule we're after must be representable as a finite automaton. Our book *Finite Automata and Regular Expressions: Problems and Solutions* goes into depth on the subject, but we will explain enough here to construct them for our purposes.

Let's say we want to generate all production rules with one or more +'s or −'s in a row, and no more than 2 F's in a row, but +'s and −'s cannot be bunched together, since they cancel each other out. The automaton for this is shown below.

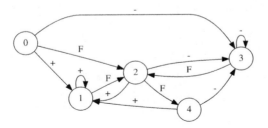

This automaton is represented in the file lsys1.aut as follows:

```
; lsys1.aut is for one or more +'s or -'s in a row,
; with no more than 2 F's in a row.
; Example: autogen lsys1.aut 4 0 2 4
;    Produces words of length 4, with start state 0,
;    and end states 2 and 4.
5
0 +1 F2 -3
1 +1 F2
2 +1 -3 F4
3 F2 -3
4 +1 -3
```

The automaton file can begin with any number of comment lines marked by a semicolon in the first column. The first non-comment line is the number of nodes (states) in the automaton, in this case 5. The second line '0 +1 F2 -3' describes the outgoing connections (edges) from node 0. Node 0 goes to node 1 on a +, goes to node 2 on a F, and goes to node 3 on a -. The third line describes the outgoing edges from node 1. Node 1 loops back to itself on a +, and goes to node 2 on a F. Likewise, each additional line describes a node's outgoing edges. The description is a two character string. The first character is an L-system symbol and the second character is a node number. The nodes can also be labeled with symbols. You could for example use lower case letters $a, b, c, d, \ldots$ to label the nodes.

Now let's ask the `autogen` program to generate for us all production rules of length 4 satisfying the above automaton, which also do not end with +'s or −'s. The command for doing this is:

`autogen lsys1.aut 4 0 2 4`

where `lsys1.aut` is the name of the input file. The first number (4) is the length of the production rules we want it to generate. The second number (0) is the start state. The last two numbers (2 4) specify the end states. A production rule will end in state 2 or 4 only if it ends with one or two F's and not with a + or −. The result of running this `autogen` command is:

```
+++F
++FF
```

```
+F+F
+F-F
F++F
F+FF
F-FF
F--F
FF+F
FF-F
-F+F
-F-F
--FF
---F
```

So autogen has generated for us 14 production rules whose L-system images we can generate using lsysgen and turtledraw. All we need is an axiom. Choosing F+F+F+F as the axiom so that that for our first production rule in the list above, we create an ldf file consisting of the following two lines:

```
F+F+F+F
F->+++F
```

Save these two lines in the file file1.ldf then run lsysgen with turtledraw as follows:

```
lsysgen file1.ldf 3 | turtledraw 0.0 90.0 file.svg
```

Note that we specified 3 steps, start angle $= 0°$ and turn angle $= 90°$. The resulting SVG file can now be viewed. The process can be repeated for each of the other 13 production rules in the list above. Some of the images generated like this are shown below.

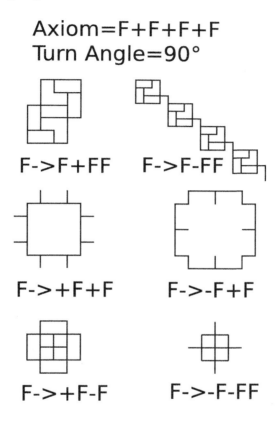

Axiom=F+F+F+F
Turn Angle=90°

F->F+FF   F->F-FF

F->+F+F   F->-F+F

F->+F-F   F->-F-FF

If we add two more $+F$'s to the axiom, making it $F + F + F + F + F + F$, and change the turn angle from 90° to 60°, we get something quite different. Some interesting ones are shown below.

Axiom=F+F+F+F+F+F
Turn Angle=60°

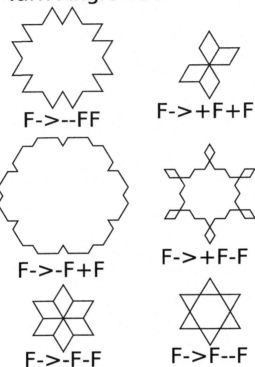

F->--FF

F->+F+F

F->-F+F

F->+F-F

F->-F-F

F->F--F

COUPLED PRODUCTION RULES

Adding another symbol G to the symbol F that was used in the last automaton, transforms that automaton into the following.

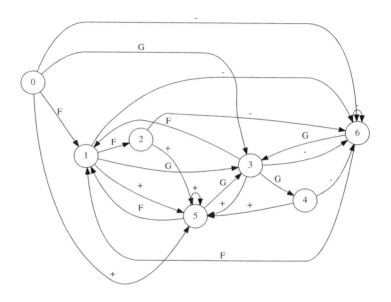

This automaton allows us to make two coupled production rule L-systems, like the Sierpinski gasket already

discussed. The automaton is represented in the file
lsys4.aut as follows:

```
; lsys4.aut is for coupled production rules
; with one or more +'s or -'s in a row, and
; no more than 2 F's or G's in a row, but
; allowing for FGG or GFF.
; Example: autogen lsys4.aut 4 0 1 2 3 4 5 6
;    Produces words of length 4, with start
;    state 0, and end states 1,2,3,4,5,6.
7
0 F1 G3 +5 -6
1 F2 G3 +5 -6
2 +5 -6
3 F1 G4 +5 -6
4 +5 -6
5 F1 G3 +5
6 F1 G3 -6
```

Now generating the length 4 production rules using this
automaton file, and specifying start state 0, with end
states 1, 2, 3, 4, 5, 6:

`autogen lsys4.aut 4 0 1 2 3 4 5 6`

The output of this autogen call produces 150 production rules, but this includes rules that have only F's
or only G's which is not wanted (we want coupling).
It also includes rules that have only letters, as well as
rules with all +'s and $-$'s, which are also not interest-

ing. So cutting those out leaves us with 76 production
rules as shown below:

```
FF+G  FF-G  FGF+  FGF-  FGG+  FGG-  FG+F  FG+G
FG++  FG-F  FG-G  FG--  F+FG  F+GF  F+GG  F+G+
F+G-  F++G  F-FG  F-GF  F-GG  F-G+  F-G-  F--G
GFF+  GFF-  GFG+  GFG-  GF+F  GF+G  GF++  GF-F
GF-G  GF--  GG+F  GG-F  G+FF  G+FG  G+F+  G+F-
G+GF  G++F  G-FF  G-FG  G-F+  G-F-  G-GF  G--F
+FGF  +FGG  +FG+  +FG-  +F+G  +F-G  +GFF  +GFG
+GF+  +GF-  +G+F  +G-F  ++FG  ++GF  -FGF  -FGG
-FG+  -FG-  -F+G  -F-G  -GFF  -GFG  -GF+  -GF-
-G+F  -G-F  --FG  --GF
```

If for each of these production rules, an `ldf` file is created with arbitrarily chosen axiom $F+F+F+F+F+F$
and the second production rule being the current production rule's inverse, we can generate images for coupled production rule L-systems. For example the first
production rule in the list above is $FF + G$, and its
inverse is $GG - F$ gotten by swapping F for G, $+$ for
$-$, and vice versa. So the `ldf` file corresponding to the
first production rule would consist of the three lines:

```
F+F+F+F+F+F
F->FF+G
G->GG-F
```

Now an image can be generated on the command line like this:

```
lsysgen file.ldf 4 | turtledraw 0.0 60.0 file.svg
```

where `file.ldf` consists of the three lines above, and steps = 4 and turn angle = 60° are arbitrarily chosen.

Similarly images can be generated for all L-systems corresponding to the 76 production rules above. Some of these are shown below.

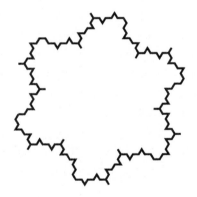

Axiom=F+F+F+F+F+F
F->FGF+
G->GFG-
Turn Angle=60°

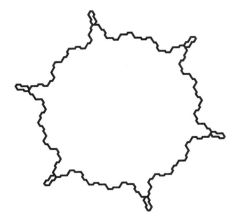

Axiom=F+F+F+F+F+F
F->FG+F
G->GF-G
Turn Angle=60°

Axiom=F+F+F+F+F+F
F->FG--
G->GF++
Turn Angle=60°

Axiom=F+F+F+F+F+F
F->F+FG
G->G-GF
Turn Angle=60°

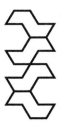

Axiom=F+F+F+F+F+F
F->F+G+
G->G-F-
Turn Angle=60°

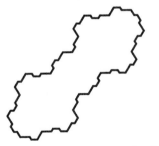

Axiom=F+F+F+F+F+F
F->F-GF
G->G+FG
Turn Angle=60°

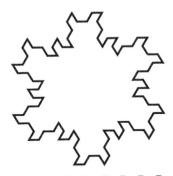

Axiom=F+F+F+F+F+F
F->F-G-
G->G+F+
Turn Angle=60°

Axiom=F+F+F+F+F+F
F->F--G
G->G++F
Turn Angle=60°

Axiom=F+F+F+F+F+F
F->GFF+
G->FGG-
Turn Angle=60°

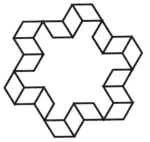

Axiom=F+F+F+F+F+F
F->G+F-
G->F-G+
Turn Angle=60°

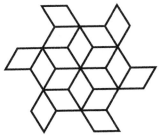

Axiom=F+F+F+F+F+F
F->G-F+
G->F+G-
Turn Angle=60°

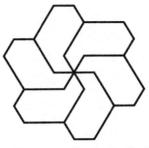

Axiom=F+F+F+F+F+F
F->G-F-
G->F+G+
Turn Angle=60°

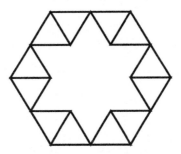

Axiom=F+F+F+F+F+F
F->+GF-
G->-FG+
Turn Angle=60°

Note that although we've reduced some redundancies as described above in going from 150 production rules to 76, there are still lots more. Redundancy can be reduced even more by removing the inverses (e.g. F+G- ↔ G-F+) and mirrors (e.g. F+G- ↔ -G+F), which in this case cuts down the number of production rules from 76 to 31.

If the turn angle is changed to 90° and axiom to $F + F + F + F$, a few of those are shown below.

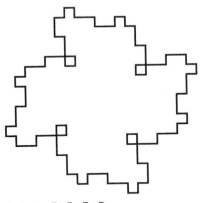

Axiom=F+F+F+F
F->FGG+
G->GFF-
Turn Angle=90°

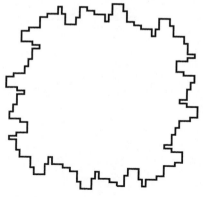

Axiom=F+F+F+F
F->FG+G-
G->GF-F
Turn Angle=90°

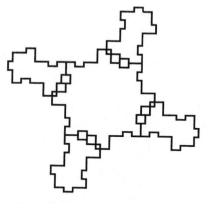

Axiom=F+F+F+F
F->FG-F
G->GF+G
Turn Angle=90°

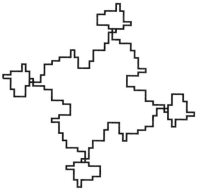

Axiom=F+F+F+F
F->FG-G
G->GF+F
Turn Angle=90°

The length 5 production rules can be gotten by changing the first number parameter of autogen to 5 like this:

autogen lsys4.aut 5 0 1 2 3 4 5 6

This outputs 494 production rules, but after removing the non-coupled ones, as well as inverses and mirrors, only 134 remain. Some of the 4th step L-systems for turn angle 60° and axiom $F + F + F + F + F + F$ are shown below.

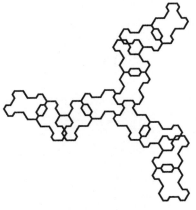

Axiom=F+F+F+F+F+F
F->F+GG
G->GG-FF
Turn Angle=60°

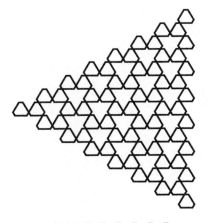

Axiom=F+F+F+F+F+F
F->GF+F
G->GFG-G
Turn Angle=60°

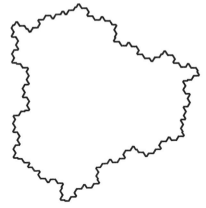

Axiom=F+F+F+F+F+F
F->FGF+G
G->GFG-F
Turn Angle=60°

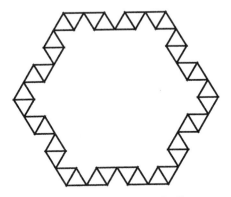

Axiom=F+F+F+F+F+F
F->FGF--
G->GFG++
Turn Angle=60°

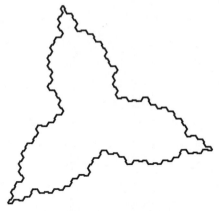

Axiom=F+F+F+F+F+F
F->FGG+F
G->GFF-G
Turn Angle=60°

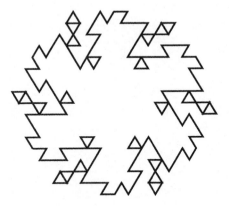

Axiom=F+F+F+F+F+F
F->FGG--
G->GFF++
Turn Angle=60°

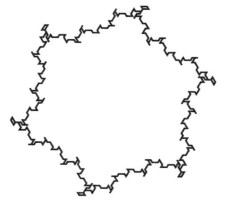

Axiom=F+F+F+F+F+F
F->FG+F-
G->GF-G+
Turn Angle=60°

Axiom=F+F+F+F+F+F
F->FG-G-
G->GF+F+
Turn Angle=60°

Axiom=F+F+F+F+F+F
F->F+F+G
G->G-G-F
Turn Angle=60°

Axiom=F+F+F+F+F+F
F->F+GFG
G->G-FGF
Turn Angle=60°

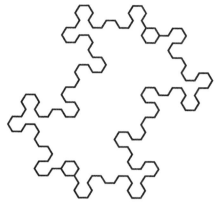

Axiom=F+F+F+F+F+F
F->F+G+F
G->G-F-G
Turn Angle=60°

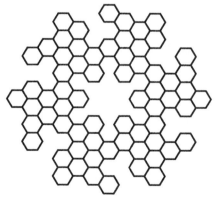

Axiom=F+F+F+F+F+F
F->F-F-G
G->G+G+F
Turn Angle=60°

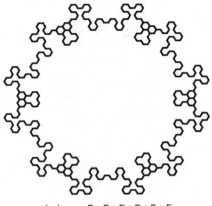

Axiom=F+F+F+F+F+F
F->F-G-F
G->G+F+G
Turn Angle=60°

For turn angle 90° and axiom $F + F + F + F$, some examples are shown below.

Axiom=F+F+F+F
F->FF-GF
G->GG+FG
Turn Angle=90°

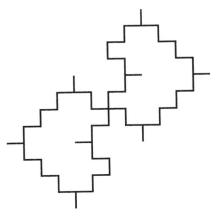

Axiom=F+F+F+F
F->FGFF-
G->GFGG+
Turn Angle=90°

Axiom=F+F+F+F
F->FG+F-
G->GF-G+
Turn Angle=90°

Axiom=F+F+F+F
F->F+G+G
G->G-F-F
Turn Angle=90°

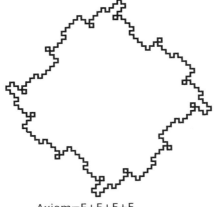

Axiom=F+F+F+F
F->F-G+G
G->G+F-F
Turn Angle=90°

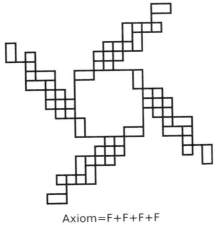

Axiom=F+F+F+F
F->+FF+G
G->-GG-F
Turn Angle=90°

Similarly, `autogen` produces 1,622 production rules of
length 6, and after removing the non-coupled ones, as
well as inverses and mirrors, 499 remain. Some of the
4th step L-systems for turn angle 60° and axiom $F +
F + F + F + F + F$ are shown below.

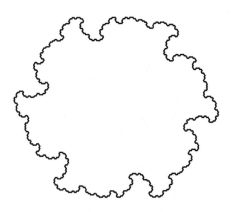

Axiom=F+F+F+F+F+F
F->FF+FG-
G->GG-GF+
Turn Angle=60°

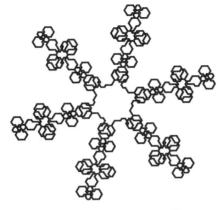

Axiom=F+F+F+F+F+F
F->FF+GFF
G->GG-FGG
Turn Angle=60°

Axiom=F+F+F+F+F+F
F->FF-FG-
G->GG+GF+
Turn Angle=60°

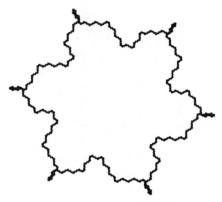

Axiom=F+F+F+F+F+F
F->FGF+GF
G->GFG-FG
Turn Angle=60°

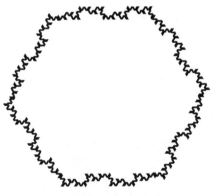

Axiom=F+F+F+F+F+F
F->FGF-G-
G->GFG+F+
Turn Angle=60°

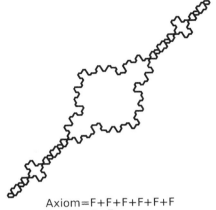

Axiom=F+F+F+F+F+F
F->FG+G+F
G->GF-F-G
Turn Angle=60°

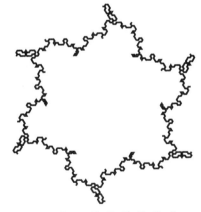

Axiom=F+F+F+F+F+F
F->FG-GF-
G->GF+FG+
Turn Angle=60°

Axiom=F+F+F+F+F+F
F->F+F+FG
G->G-G-GF
Turn Angle=60°

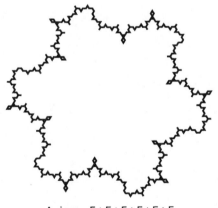

Axiom=F+F+F+F+F+F
F->F+G-F+
G->G-F+G-
Turn Angle=60°

Axiom=F+F+F+F+F+F
F->F++F-G
G->G--G+F
Turn Angle=60°

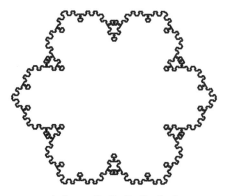

Axiom=F+F+F+F+F+F
F->F--G-F
G->G++F+G
Turn Angle=60°

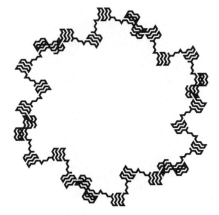

Axiom=F+F+F+F+F+F
F->+FGFGG
G->-GFGFF
Turn Angle=60°

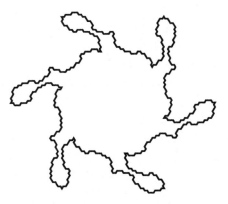

Axiom=F+F+F+F+F+F
F->+F-F+G
G->-G+G-F
Turn Angle=60°

Axiom=F+F+F+F+F+F
F->+G+F-G
G->-F-G+F
Turn Angle=60°

For turn angle 90° and axiom $F + F + F + F$, some examples are shown below.

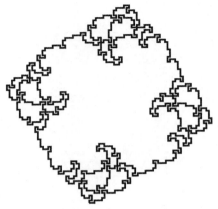

Axiom=F+F+F+F
F->FF+F-G
G->GG-G+F
Turn Angle=90°

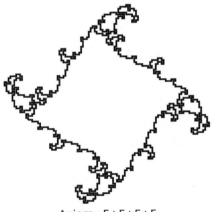

Axiom=F+F+F+F
F->FF-F+G
G->GG+G-F
Turn Angle=90°

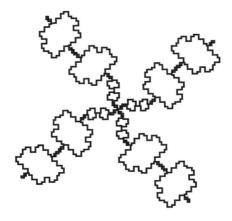

Axiom=F+F+F+F
F->FGG+GF
G->GFF-FG
Turn Angle=90°

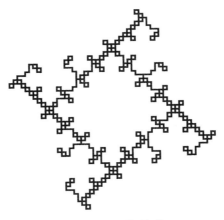

Axiom=F+F+F+F
F->FG+GFG
G->GF-FGF
Turn Angle=90°

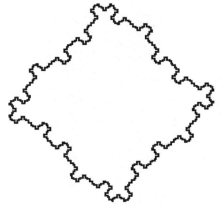

Axiom=F+F+F+F
F->FG-G+F
G->GF+F-G
Turn Angle=90°

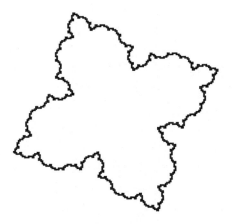

Axiom=F+F+F+F
F->F+GG+F
G->G-FF-G
Turn Angle=90°

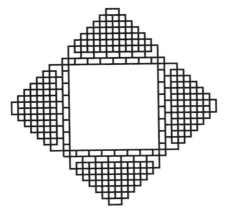

Axiom=F+F+F+F
F->F-GF+G
G->G+FG-F
Turn Angle=90°

BRANCHING

Branching in an L-system allows us to remember the current position, then go off and do something, and finally come back to our remembered position. This can result in L-systems that look plant-like.

We'll use a left square bracket '[' to indicate the start of a branch and the position to be remembered, then a right square bracket ']' for going back to the last position remembered.

If we start with axiom F and use the production rule $F \to F[A][B]F$ where A is a string that starts with a '+' sign followed by any combination of F's, +'s and -'s, while B is the inverse of A (+'s swapped for -'s and vice versa), then we will have a symmetric tree-like L-system as shown below for turn angle = 30° and $F \to F[+F][-F]F$.

For production rule $F \to F[A]F[B]F$, the branches will alternate left to right as shown below for $F \to F[+F]F[-F]F$.

These are two basic forms of a tree. A variety of trees can be made by simply using different A strings. Our program `cfgen`, which stands for context free grammar generator, can be used to generate the A string.

`cfgen` takes as input a context free grammar definition file, followed by the number of steps to iterate, and finally the start state. For example, if we run `cfgen` like this:

`cfgen lsys0.cfg 10 A`

we are telling `cfgen` to read the context free grammar definition file `lsys0.cfg`, iterating it 10 steps, and using start state `A`, where `lsys0.cfg` is composed of the following lines:

```
2
A SFA SF
S + - ++ --
```

The first line of the file contains a single number, in this case 2, indicating that there are 2 grammar rules to follow. The second line, 'A SFA SF' is the first grammar rule, stating that A can become SFA or SF. The third line, 'S + - ++ --' states that S can become any of the four signs or sign combinations + - ++ --. For example, in the first step, we begin with start state A. Let's say A becomes SFA, and S becomes -, so now we have -FA. In the second step, let's say the A in -FA becomes SF, so that -FA becomes -FSF. Now if S becomes +, then we are left with -F+F. Since there are no more A's remaining, the iteration stops. The output of cfgen is all possible strings (also called words) constructed in this way. For our purposes here, we can use this output as the *A* string mentioned above to systematically look at the varieties of possible trees. Some of these trees are shown below (chosen from the 1,364 *A* strings produced by the cfgen command above).

Axiom=F
F->F[A]F[B]F
A=+F--F++F-F+F
B=-F++F--F+F-F
Turn Angle=30°
Steps=3

Axiom=F
F->F[A]F[B]F
A=+F-F+F-F+F
B=-F+F-F+F-F
Turn Angle=30°
Steps=3

Axiom=F
F->F[A]F[B]F
A=+F
B=-F
Turn Angle=30°
Steps=3

Axiom=F
F->F[A]F[B]F
A=+F+F+F+F-F
B=-F-F-F-F+F
Turn Angle=30°
Steps=3

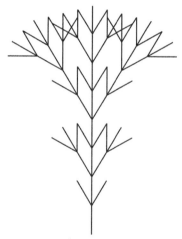

Axiom=F
F->F[A][B]F
A=+F
B=-F
Turn Angle=30°
Steps=3

Axiom=F
F->F[A][B]F
A=+F-F-F
B=-F+F+F
Turn Angle=30°
Steps=3

Axiom=F
F->F[A][B]F
A=++F-F-F--F++F
B=--F+F+F++F--F
Turn Angle=30°
Steps=3

Axiom=F
F->F[A][B]F
A=++F--F+F+F++F
B=--F++F-F-F--F
Turn Angle=30°
Steps=3

Axiom=F
F->F[A]F[B]F
A=+F+F
B=-F-F
Turn Angle=30°
Steps=3

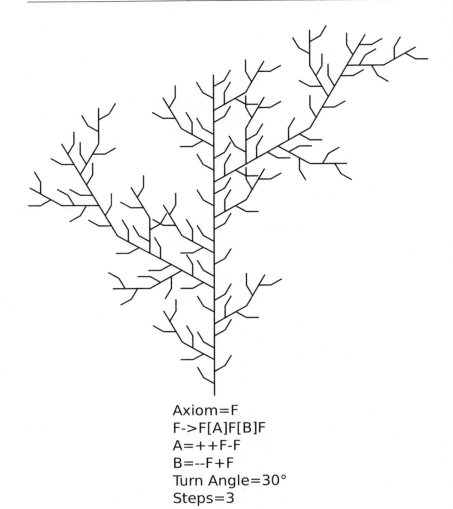

Axiom=F
F->F[A]F[B]F
A=++F-F
B=--F+F
Turn Angle=30°
Steps=3

Axiom=F
F->F[A]F[B]F
A=+F+F-F+F
B=-F-F+F-F
Turn Angle=30°
Steps=3

Axiom=F
F->F[A][B]F
A=+F-F+F--F
B=-F+F-F++F++F
Turn Angle=30°
Steps=3

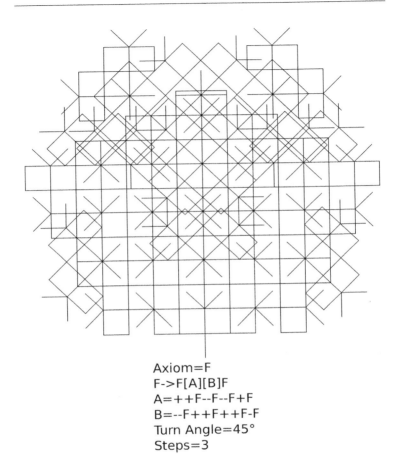

Axiom=F
F->F[A][B]F
A=++F--F--F+F
B=--F++F++F-F
Turn Angle=45°
Steps=3

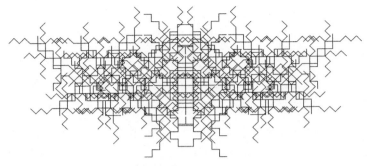

Axiom=F
F->F[A][B]F
A=++F-F++F--F++F
B=--F+F--F++F--F
Turn Angle=45°
Steps=3

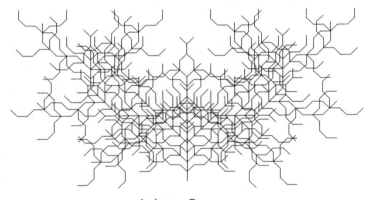

Axiom=F
F->F[A][B]F
A=+F+F-F-F
B=-F-F+F+F
Turn Angle=45°
Steps=3

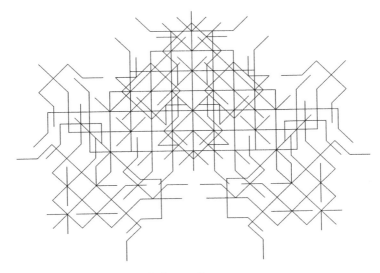

Axiom=F
F->F[A][B]F
A=++F++F-F
B=--F--F+F
Turn Angle=45°
Steps=3

Axiom=F
F->F[A][B]F
A=+F--F--F--F++F
B=-F++F++F++F--F
Turn Angle=45°
Steps=3

Axiom=F
F->F[A][B]F
A=++F++F++F+F
B=--F--F--F-F
Turn Angle=45°
Steps=3

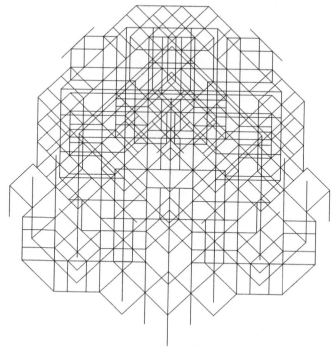

Axiom=F
F->F[A][B]F
A=+F--F--F-F
B=-F++F++F+F
Turn Angle=45°
Steps=3

Axiom=F
F->F[A][B]F
A=++F+F+F++F+F
B=--F-F-F--F-F
Turn Angle=45°
Steps=3

Axiom=F
F->F[A][B]F
A=+F--F--F--F+F
B=-F++F++F++F-F
Turn Angle=45°
Steps=3

Axiom=F
F->F[A][B]F
A=+F-F--F--F++F
B=-F+F++F++F--F
Turn Angle=45°
Steps=3

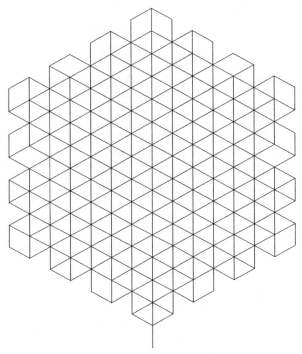

Axiom=F
F->F[A][B]F
A=+F--F+F--F-F
B=-F++F-F++F+F
Turn Angle=60°
Steps=3

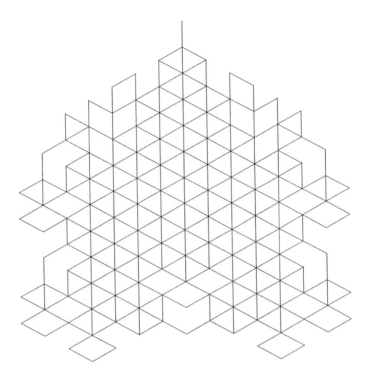

Axiom=F
F->F[A][B]F
A=++F++F--F++F
B=--F--F++F--F
Turn Angle=60°
Steps=3

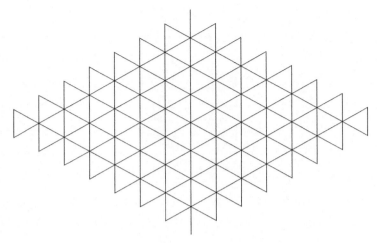

Axiom=F
F->F[A][B]F
A=++F--F--F-F
B=--F++F++F+F
Turn Angle=60°
Steps=3

Axiom=F
F->F[A][B]F
A=+F+F--F++F
B=-F-F++F--F
Turn Angle=60°
Steps=3

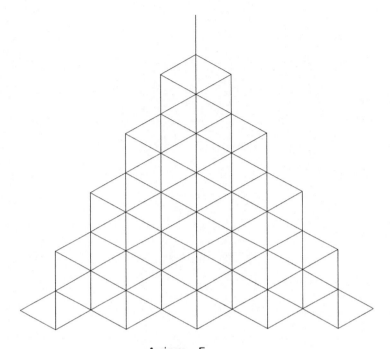

Axiom=F
F->F[A][B]F
A=++F++F
B=--F--F
Turn Angle=60°
Steps=3

Axiom=F
F->F[A]F[B]F
A=++F--F++F+F--F
B=--F++F--F-F++F
Turn Angle=90°
Steps=3

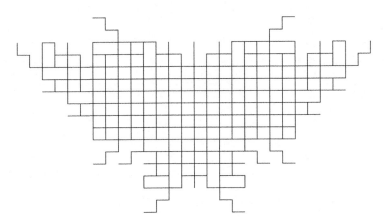

Axiom=F
F->F[A][B]F
A=++F+F+F-F+F
B=--F-F-F+F-F
Turn Angle=90°
Steps=3

Axiom=F
F->F[A]F[B]F
A=+F++F-F++F-F
B=-F--F+F--F+F
Turn Angle=90°
Steps=3

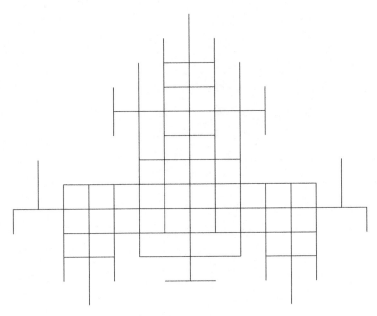

Axiom=F
F->F[A][B]F
A=++F++F++F+F-F
B=--F--F--F-F+F
Turn Angle=90°
Steps=3

Axiom=F
F->F[A]F[B]F
A=+F--F++F+F--F
B=-F++F--F-F++F
Turn Angle=15°
Steps=3

Axiom=F
F->F[A][B]F
A=+F--F++F--F+F
B=-F++F--F++F-F
Turn Angle=15°
Steps=3

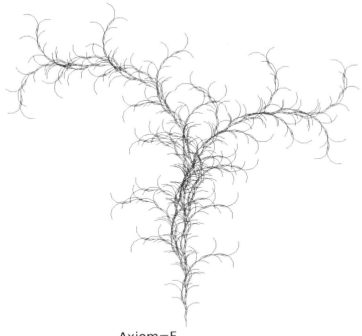

Axiom=F
F->F[A]F[B]F
A=+F--F-F--F
B=-F++F+F++F++F
Turn Angle=15°
Steps=3

Axiom=F
F->F[A]F[B]F
A=++F-F+F-F+F
B=--F+F-F+F-F
Turn Angle=15°
Steps=3

Axiom=F
F->F[A]F[B]F
A=++F++F--F+F-F
B=--F--F++F-F+F
Turn Angle=15°
Steps=3

Axiom=F
F->F[A]F[B]F
A=++F-F-F--F++F
B=--F+F+F++F--F
Turn Angle=15°
Steps=3

Axiom=F
F->F[A]F[B]F
A=++F++F-F--F-F
B=--F--F+F++F+F
Turn Angle=15°
Steps=3

Axiom=F
F->F[A]F[B]F
A=+F-F+F+F
B=-F+F-F-F
Turn Angle=15°
Steps=3

Axiom=F
F->F[A][B]F
A=++F+F--F--F-F
B=--F-F++F++F+F
Turn Angle=15°
Steps=3

Axiom=F
F->F[A][B]F
A=++F-F-F++F
B=--F+F+F--F
Turn Angle=15°
Steps=3

Axiom=F
F->F[A][B]F
A=+F++F++F+F+F
B=-F--F--F-F-F
Turn Angle=17°
Steps=3

Axiom=F
F->F[A][B]F
A=++F--F-F+F-F
B=--F++F+F-F+F
Turn Angle=17°
Steps=3

Axiom=F
F->F[A]F[B]F
A=++F++F+F+F+F
B=--F--F-F-F-F
Turn Angle=7°
Steps=3

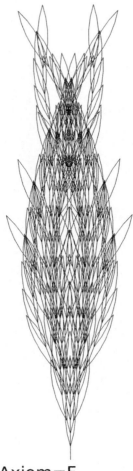

Axiom=F
F->F[A][B]F
A=++F-F-F-F-F
B=--F+F+F+F+F
Turn Angle=7°
Steps=3

APPENDIX A: KATRANS
AUTOMATON FILES

This appendix lists automaton files used to generate the images in this book. They can be downloaded from the book's web page (link).

You can use these automata files to translate any binary string with the program **katrans** that can be downloaded from the book's web page (link).

t0.kat is a simple automaton that turns a 0 into F and 1 into $+F$. t0a,b,c.kat are just variations on the output symbols of t0.kat.

t0.kat

```
3 2
0 1 2
1 1 2 F
2 1 2 +F
```

t0a.kat

```
3 2
0 1 2
1 1 2 +
2 1 2 F+F--F+F
```

t0b.kat

```
3 2
0 1 2
1 1 2 F+F+F+F+F+F
2 1 2 F+F--F+F
```

t0c.kat

```
3 2
0 1 2
1 1 2 +
2 1 2 F+F-F-FF+F+F-F
```

The following 3 automata (t1,2,3.kat) files represented in figure 14 are all the same except for drawing instructions (output strings). They differentiate whether a 0 or 1 is at an even or odd position. A 0 at an even position puts the automaton in state 1 and a 0 at an odd position puts it in state 4. A 1 at an even position puts the automaton in state 3 and a 1 at an odd position puts it in state 2.

t1.kat

```
; 1-bit parity
;state 0 = start
;state 1 = have a 0 at an even position
;state 2 = have a 1 at an odd position
```

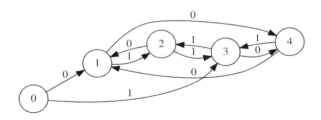

Figure 14: 1-bit parity automaton

```
;state 3 = have a 1 at an even position
;state 4 = have a 0 at an odd position
5 2
0 1 3
1 4 2 F
2 1 3 +F
3 4 2 -F
4 1 3 F
```

t2.kat

```
;  1-bit parity
;state 0 = start
;state 1 = have a 0 at an even position
;state 2 = have a 1 at an odd position
;state 3 = have a 1 at an even position
;state 4 = have a 0 at an odd position
```

```
5 2
0 1 3
1 4 2 F
2 1 3 +F
3 4 2 F
4 1 3 -F
```

t3.kat

```
; 1-bit parity
;state 0 = start
;state 1 = have a 0 at an even position
;state 2 = have a 1 at an odd position
;state 3 = have a 1 at an even position
;state 4 = have a 0 at an odd position
5 2
0 1 3
1 4 2 +F
2 1 3 F
3 4 2 -F
4 1 3 F
```

t4.kat represented in figure 15 was designed to differentiate if a 0 or 1 is at a position number whose remainder after dividing by 3 is 0, 1 or 2. These positions are labeled as 0 mod 3, 1 mod 3, and 2 mod 3. States 1 − 3 correspond to 0's at 0 mod 3, 1 mod 3, and 2 mod 3 respectively. States 4 − 6 correspond to 1's at 0 mod 3, 1 mod 3, and 2 mod 3 respectively.

For example if there's a 1 at position 5 then the automaton will be in state 6 since 5 leaves a remainder of 2 after division by 3 so the position is 2 mod 3.

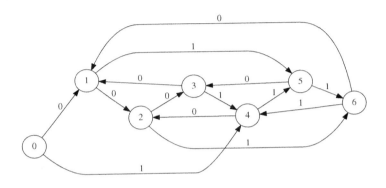

Figure 15: 1-bit 3-positions automaton

`t4.kat`

```
; 1-bit 3-positions
;state 0 = start
;state 1 = have a 0 at a position 0 modulo 3
;state 2 = have a 0 at a position 1 modulo 3
;state 3 = have a 0 at a position 2 modulo 3
;state 4 = have a 1 at a position 0 modulo 3
;state 5 = have a 1 at a position 1 modulo 3
;state 6 = have a 1 at a position 2 modulo 3
7 2
0 1 4
```

```
1 2 5 +F
2 3 6 -F-F
3 1 4 -F
4 2 5 -FF
5 3 6 +F+F
6 1 4 +FF
```

The following 6 automata (t5,6,7,8,9,10.kat) files represented in figure 16 are all the same except for drawing instructions. The automaton was designed to count runs up to length 2. For example, after reading the first 0, we have a 0 run of length 1. If the next number is also a 0, then we have a run of length 2. If the next number is again a 0, then the run count resets to 1. State 1 corresponds to a 0 with run count 1. State 2 corresponds to a 1 with run count 1. State 3 to a 0 with run count 2, and state 4 to a 1 with run count 2.

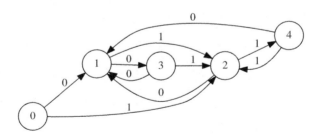

Figure 16: Count run lengths up to 2 automaton

t5.kat

```
; counts runs up to length 2
;state 0 = start
;state 1 = have a 0 with run count 1
;state 2 = have a 1 with run count 1
;state 3 = have a 0 with run count 2
;state 4 = have a 1 with run count 2
5 2
0 1 2
1 3 2 -F
2 1 4 -F
3 1 2 +F
4 1 2 f
```

t6.kat

```
; counts runs up to length 2
;state 0 = start
;state 1 = have a 0 with run count 1
;state 2 = have a 1 with run count 1
;state 3 = have a 0 with run count 2
;state 4 = have a 1 with run count 2
5 2
0 1 2
1 3 2 F++F++F++F
2 1 4 -FF+FFFF+FF
3 1 2 FF-FF+FF
4 1 2 f
```

t7.kat

```
; counts runs up to length 2
;state 0 = start
;state 1 = have a 0 with run count 1
;state 2 = have a 1 with run count 1
;state 3 = have a 0 with run count 2
;state 4 = have a 1 with run count 2
5 2
0 1 2
1 3 2 F+FF+F
2 1 4 +FFF+
3 1 2 F-F
4 1 2 -FF
```

t8.kat

```
; counts runs up to length 2
;state 0 = start
;state 1 = have a 0 with run count 1
;state 2 = have a 1 with run count 1
;state 3 = have a 0 with run count 2
;state 4 = have a 1 with run count 2
5 2
0 1 2
1 3 2 F+FFF+F
2 1 4 +FFF+
3 1 2 F-F
4 1 2 FF
```

```
t9.kat


; counts runs up to length 2
;state 0 = start
;state 1 = have a 0 with run count 1
;state 2 = have a 1 with run count 1
;state 3 = have a 0 with run count 2
;state 4 = have a 1 with run count 2
5 2
0 1 2
1 3 2 +F-F+
2 1 4 F++F
3 1 2 F-
4 1 2 -F


t10.kat


; counts runs up to length 2
;state 0 = start
;state 1 = have a 0 with run count 1
;state 2 = have a 1 with run count 1
;state 3 = have a 0 with run count 2
;state 4 = have a 1 with run count 2
5 2
0 1 2
1 3 2 +F-F+
2 1 4 F++F
3 1 2 +F
4 1 2 -F
```

The following 2 automata (t11,12.kat) files represented in figure 17 are the same except for drawing instructions. They are like the last 6 files, except they count runs up to length 3.

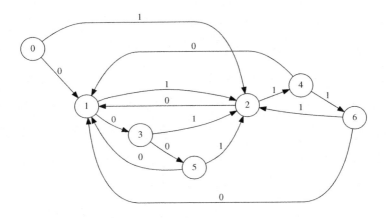

Figure 17: Count run lengths up to 3 automaton

`t11.kat`

```
; counts runs up to length 3
;state 0 = start
;state 1 = have a 0 with run count 1
;state 2 = have a 1 with run count 1
;state 3 = have a 0 with run count 2
;state 4 = have a 1 with run count 2
;state 5 = have a 0 with run count 3
```

```
;state 6 = have a 1 with run count 3
7 2
0 1 2
1 3 2 F--F
2 1 4 -FF-
3 5 2 FF+
4 1 6 +FF
5 1 2 +FFF
6 1 2 FFF+
```

t12.kat

```
; counts runs up to length 3
;state 0 = start
;state 1 = have a 0 with run count 1
;state 2 = have a 1 with run count 1
;state 3 = have a 0 with run count 2
;state 4 = have a 1 with run count 2
;state 5 = have a 0 with run count 3
;state 6 = have a 1 with run count 3
7 2
0 1 2
1 3 2 F--F
2 1 4 -F-F
3 5 2 -FF+
4 1 6 +FF-
5 1 2 +FFF
6 1 2 FFF+
```

The following 3 automata (t{13,14,15}.kat) files represented in figures 18, 19 and 20 are based on de Bruijn graphs. You can simply use them as they are. The theory behind them can be found on *Wikipedia*.

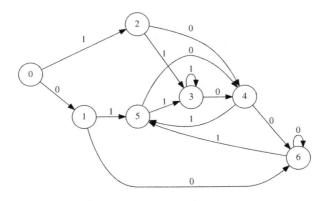

Figure 18: 2-bit de Bruijn graph automaton

t13.kat

```
; 2-bit de Bruijn graph
7 2
0 1 2
1 6 5
2 4 3
3 4 3 +F
4 6 5 -F
5 4 3 -F
6 6 5 +F
```

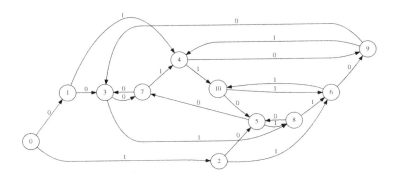

Figure 19: 2-bit de Bruijn graph with parity split automaton

t14.kat

```
; 2-bit de Bruijn graph with parity split
11 2
0 1 2
1 3 4 +F
2 5 6 +F
3 7 8 -F
4 9 10 +F
5 7 8 +F
6 9 10 -F
7 3 4 +F
8 5 6 -F
9 3 4 -F
10 5 6 +F
```

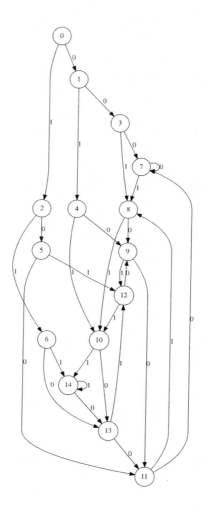

Figure 20: 3-bit de Bruijn graph automaton

`t15.kat`

```
; 3-bit de Bruijn graph
15 2
0 1 2
1 3 4
2 5 6
3 7 8
4 9 10
5 11 12
6 13 14
7 7 8 -F
8 9 10 +F
9 11 12 +F
10 13 14 +F
11 7 8 -F
12 9 10 -F
13 11 12 +F
14 13 14 -F
```

Paper folding automaton

The following automaton file is intended for use with the output of program `pfold`. It contains drawing instructions so that the drawing will resemble the actual shape of the unfolded paper by converting a 1 to $-F$ and a 0 to $+F$. If you use a turn angle of 90 degrees then the drawing will look like the shape of the paper

when each fold is unfolded to 90 degrees and you are
looking at the paper edge on.

pf0.kat

```
; Paper folding
3 2
0 2 1
1 2 1 +F
2 2 1 -F
```

APPENDIX B: CONTINUED FRACTIONS

$$\sqrt{2} = [1, \overline{2}]$$
$$\sqrt{3} = [1, \overline{1, 2}]$$
$$\sqrt{5} = [2, \overline{4}]$$
$$\sqrt{6} = [2, \overline{2, 4}]$$
$$\sqrt{7} = [2, \overline{1, 1, 1, 4}]$$
$$\sqrt{8} = [2, \overline{1, 4}]$$
$$\sqrt{10} = [3, \overline{6}]$$
$$\sqrt{11} = [3, \overline{3, 6}]$$
$$\sqrt{12} = [3, \overline{2, 6}]$$
$$\sqrt{13} = [3, \overline{1, 1, 1, 1, 6}]$$
$$\sqrt{14} = [3, \overline{1, 2, 1, 6}]$$
$$\sqrt{15} = [3, \overline{1, 6}]$$
$$\sqrt{17} = [4, \overline{8}]$$
$$\sqrt{18} = [4, \overline{4, 8}]$$
$$\sqrt{19} = [4, \overline{2, 1, 3, 1, 2, 8}]$$
$$\sqrt{20} = [4, \overline{2, 8}]$$
$$\sqrt{21} = [4, \overline{1, 1, 2, 1, 1, 8}]$$
$$\sqrt{22} = [4, \overline{1, 2, 4, 2, 1, 8}]$$
$$\sqrt{23} = [4, \overline{1, 3, 1, 8}]$$
$$\sqrt{24} = [4, \overline{1, 8}]$$
$$\sqrt{26} = [5, \overline{10}]$$
$$\sqrt{27} = [5, \overline{5, 10}]$$
$$\sqrt{28} = [5, \overline{3, 2, 3, 10}]$$
$$\sqrt{29} = [5, \overline{2, 1, 1, 2, 10}]$$
$$\sqrt{30} = [5, \overline{2, 10}]$$
$$\sqrt{31} = [5, \overline{1, 1, 3, 5, 3, 1, 1, 10}]$$
$$\sqrt{32} = [5, \overline{1, 1, 1, 10}]$$
$$\sqrt{33} = [5, \overline{1, 2, 1, 10}]$$
$$\sqrt{34} = [5, \overline{1, 4, 1, 10}]$$
$$\sqrt{35} = [5, \overline{1, 10}]$$

$$\sqrt{37} = [6, \overline{12}]$$
$$\sqrt{38} = [6, \overline{6, 12}]$$
$$\sqrt{39} = [6, \overline{4, 12}]$$
$$\sqrt{40} = [6, \overline{3, 12}]$$
$$\sqrt{41} = [6, \overline{2, 2, 12}]$$
$$\sqrt{42} = [6, \overline{2, 12}]$$
$$\sqrt{43} = [6, \overline{1, 1, 3, 1, 5, 1, 3, 1, 1, 12}]$$
$$\sqrt{44} = [6, \overline{1, 1, 1, 2, 1, 1, 1, 12}]$$
$$\sqrt{45} = [6, \overline{1, 2, 2, 2, 1, 12}]$$
$$\sqrt{46} = [6, \overline{1, 3, 1, 1, 2, 6, 2, 1, 1, 3, 1, 12}]$$
$$\sqrt{47} = [6, \overline{1, 5, 1, 12}]$$
$$\sqrt{48} = [6, \overline{1, 12}]$$
$$\sqrt{50} = [7, \overline{14}]$$
$$\sqrt{51} = [7, \overline{7, 14}]$$
$$\sqrt{52} = [7, \overline{4, 1, 2, 1, 4, 14}]$$
$$\sqrt{53} = [7, \overline{3, 1, 1, 3, 14}]$$
$$\sqrt{54} = [7, \overline{2, 1, 6, 1, 2, 14}]$$
$$\sqrt{55} = [7, \overline{2, 2, 2, 14}]$$
$$\sqrt{56} = [7, \overline{2, 14}]$$
$$\sqrt{57} = [7, \overline{1, 1, 4, 1, 1, 14}]$$
$$\sqrt{58} = [7, \overline{1, 1, 1, 1, 1, 1, 1, 14}]$$
$$\sqrt{59} = [7, \overline{1, 2, 7, 2, 1, 14}]$$
$$\sqrt{60} = [7, \overline{1, 2, 1, 14}]$$
$$\sqrt{61} = [7, \overline{1, 4, 3, 1, 2, 2, 1, 3, 4, 1, 14}]$$
$$\sqrt{62} = [7, \overline{1, 6, 1, 14}]$$
$$\sqrt{63} = [7, \overline{1, 14}]$$
$$\sqrt{65} = [8, \overline{16}]$$
$$\sqrt{66} = [8, \overline{8, 16}]$$
$$\sqrt{67} = [8, \overline{5, 2, 1, 1, 7, 1, 1, 2, 5, 16}]$$
$$\sqrt{68} = [8, \overline{4, 16}]$$

$$\sqrt{69} = [8, \overline{3, 3, 1, 4, 1, 3, 3, 16}]$$
$$\sqrt{70} = [8, \overline{2, 1, 2, 1, 2, 16}]$$
$$\sqrt{71} = [8, \overline{2, 2, 1, 7, 1, 2, 2, 16}]$$
$$\sqrt{72} = [8, \overline{2, 16}]$$
$$\sqrt{73} = [8, \overline{1, 1, 5, 5, 1, 1, 16}]$$
$$\sqrt{74} = [8, \overline{1, 1, 1, 1, 16}]$$
$$\sqrt{75} = [8, \overline{1, 1, 1, 16}]$$
$$\sqrt{76} = [8, \overline{1, 2, 1, 1, 5, 4, 5, 1, 1, 2, 1, 16}]$$
$$\sqrt{77} = [8, \overline{1, 3, 2, 3, 1, 16}]$$
$$\sqrt{78} = [8, \overline{1, 4, 1, 16}]$$
$$\sqrt{79} = [8, \overline{1, 7, 1, 16}]$$
$$\sqrt{80} = [8, \overline{1, 16}]$$
$$\sqrt{82} = [9, \overline{18}]$$
$$\sqrt{83} = [9, \overline{9, 18}]$$
$$\sqrt{84} = [9, \overline{6, 18}]$$
$$\sqrt{85} = [9, \overline{4, 1, 1, 4, 18}]$$
$$\sqrt{86} = [9, \overline{3, 1, 1, 1, 8, 1, 1, 1, 3, 18}]$$
$$\sqrt{87} = [9, \overline{3, 18}]$$
$$\sqrt{88} = [9, \overline{2, 1, 1, 1, 2, 18}]$$
$$\sqrt{89} = [9, \overline{2, 3, 3, 2, 18}]$$
$$\sqrt{90} = [9, \overline{2, 18}]$$
$$\sqrt{91} = [9, \overline{1, 1, 5, 1, 5, 1, 1, 18}]$$
$$\sqrt{92} = [9, \overline{1, 1, 2, 4, 2, 1, 1, 18}]$$
$$\sqrt{93} = [9, \overline{1, 1, 1, 4, 6, 4, 1, 1, 1, 18}]$$
$$\sqrt{94} = [9, \overline{1, 2, 3, 1, 1, 5, 1, 8, 1, 5, 1, 1, 3, 2, 1, 18}]$$
$$\sqrt{95} = [9, \overline{1, 2, 1, 18}]$$
$$\sqrt{96} = [9, \overline{1, 3, 1, 18}]$$
$$\sqrt{97} = [9, \overline{1, 5, 1, 1, 1, 1, 1, 1, 5, 1, 18}]$$
$$\sqrt{98} = [9, \overline{1, 8, 1, 18}]$$
$$\sqrt{99} = [9, \overline{1, 18}]$$

APPENDIX C: PROGRAMS

autogen

> Generates all words of a given length
> accepted by an automaton
> Usage: autogen file.aut n s e1 e2 ...
>   file.aut = automaton file
>   n = length of words
>   s = start state
>   ei = end state i

b2d

> Converts a binary number to decimal
> Usage: d2b n

cfcv

> Calculates the convergent of a continued
> fraction
> Usage: cfcv a0 a1 a2 ... an
>   ai = simple continued fraction term

cfgen

> Generates the words of a context free
> grammar
> Usage: cfgen file.cfg n s

```
file.cfg  = grammar file
n = number of derivation steps
s = start variable
```

cfrac

```
Calculates the continued fraction of a real
number
Usage: cfrac x n
x = number
n = number of terms
```

cfrat

```
Calculates the continued fraction of the
rational number p/q
Usage: cfrat p q
```

cfsqrt

```
Calculates the continued fraction of the
square root of an integer
Usage: cfsqrt n
n = integer
```

cfsurd

```
Calculates the continued fraction of a
quadratic surd: (A+sqrt(n))/B where
n, A and B are integers and n>0
Usage: cfsurd n A B
n, A, B = integers, with n>0
```

chseq

Calculates a Christoffel sequence
Usage: chseq p q n
  p = numerator
  q = denominator
  n = number of terms to generate,
    default=p+q

d2b

Converts a decimal number to binary
Usage: d2b n

katrans

Translates a sequence of the numbers
 0 to k
Usage: katrans file.kat
  file.kat = k-automaton file

lsysgen

Generates an L-system string given an
axiom and set of production rules
Usage: lsysgen file.ldf n
  file.ldf = name of file with axiom
            and production rules.
  n = number of times to iterate.

pfold

Generates paper folding sequences
Usage: pfold n m f
    n = number of terms,
        1,3,7,15,31,63,127,...
    m = number of bits
    f = function number 0 -> 2^m-1

rndseq

Generates random binary sequences
Usage: rndseq n
    n = number of digits to generate

rsseq

Generates the Rudin-Shapiro sequence
Usage: rsseq n
    n = number of terms

tmseq

Generates the Thue-Morse sequence
Usage: tmseq n
    n = number of terms

turtledraw

Creates an svg file from turtle drawing
 instructions
Usage: turtledraw angle dangle file.svg
  angle = start angle
  dangle = increment angle
  file.svg = output svg file.
Example: turtledraw 0.0 30.0 koch.svg

FURTHER READING

- *Turtle Geometry: The Computer as a Medium for Exploring Mathematics*, Abelson and diSessa, 1986

- *Automatic Sequences: Theory, Applications, Generalizations*, Allouche and Shallit, 2003

- *Combinatorics on Words: Christoffel Words and Repetitions in Words (CRM Monograph)*, Berstel and Lauve and Reutenauer and Saliola, 2009

- *Fractals for the Classroom / Part Two, Complex Systems and Mandelbrot Set*, Peitgen and Jürgens and Saupe, 1992

- *The Algorithmic Beauty of Plants*, Prusinkiewicz and Lindenmayer, 1990

- *L-System Wikipedia page*

- *Pattern Wikipedia page*

- *Turtle Graphics Wikipedia page*

ACKNOWLEDGMENTS

In ordinary life we hardly realize that we receive a great deal more than we give, and that it is only with gratitude that life becomes rich. It is very easy to overestimate the importance of our own achievements in comparison with what we owe to others.

Dietrich Bonhoeffer, letter to parents from prison, Sept. 13, 1943

We'd like to thank our parents for helping us in many ways.

We thank the makers and maintainers of all the software we've used in the production of this book, including: the Emacs text editor, the LaTex typesetting system, LaTeXML, Inkscape, Evince document viewer, POV-Ray, Maxima computer algebra system, gcc, Guile, awk, sed, bash shell, and the Linux operating system.

ABOUT THE AUTHORS

Stefan Hollos and **J. Richard Hollos** are physicists by training, and enjoy anything related to math, physics, and computing. They are the authors of

- **Finite Automata and Regular Expressions: Problems and Solutions**

- **Probability Problems and Solutions**

- **Combinatorics Problems and Solutions**

- **The Coin Toss: The Hydrogen Atom of Probability**

- **Pairs Trading: A Bayesian Example**

- **Simple Trading Strategies That Work**

- **Bet Smart: The Kelly System for Gambling and Investing**

- **The QuantWolf Guide to Calculating Bond Default Probabilities**

- **The Mathematics of Lotteries: How to Calculate the Odds**

- **Signals from the Subatomic World: How to Build a Proton Precession Magnetometer**

They are brothers and business partners at Exstrom Laboratories LLC in Longmont, Colorado. Their website is exstrom.com

THANK YOU

Thank you for buying this book.

Sign up for the Abrazol Publishing Newsletter and receive news on updates, new books, and special offers. Just go to

http://www.abrazol.com/

and enter your email address.

Printed in Great Britain
by Amazon

75478427R00224